Indian Bishop
of the West

Indian Bishop of the West

The Story of Vital Justin Grandin
1829–1902

By
Frank J. Dolphin

NOVALIS

The author and publisher gratefully acknowledge the assistance of the Vital Grandin Centre, St. Albert, Alberta, and the historical advice of Rev. Claude Champagne, OMI, St. Paul University, Ottawa.

Imprimatur:

J. N. MacNeil, Archbishop of Edmonton

Cover, design and layout:

Gilles Lépine

Back-cover photo:

courtesy Canadian Broadcasting Corporation

Distributed by:

Novalis

P.O. Box 9700, Terminal
Ottawa, Ontario   K1G 4B4

Vital Grandin Centre

5 St. Vital Avenue
St. Albert, Alberta   T8N 1K1

Printed in Canada

ISBN 2-89088-277-2

NOVALIS

Canadian Cataloguing in Publication Data

Dolphin, Frank J. (Frank Joseph), 1928-
  Indian bishop of the west

Includes index.
Bibliography: p.
ISBN 2-89088-277-2

1. Grandin, Vital Justin, 1829-1902.
2. Catholic Church--Bishops--Biography.
3. Bishops--Northwest, Canadian--Biography.
4. Missionaries--Northwest, Canadian--
Biography. 5. Indians of North America--
Northwest, Canadian--Missions. 6. Oblates
of Mary Immaculate--Biography. 7. Oblates
of Mary Immaculate--Missions--Northwest,
Canadian. I. Title.

BV2813.G7D64 1986   266'.2'0924   C86-090283-8

Contents

List of Illustrations

Map

Foreword

Vital Grandin is not unknown among Catholics. The Church has already recognized him as a possible candidate for sainthood. There have been three lengthy biographies published in French and a number of articles in English. This book by Frank Dolphin, the first full-length biography to originate in English, has the merit of having been written for popular consumption.

Indian Bishop of the West should arouse a new interest in the colorful life and accomplishments of one of the first missionaries who helped establish the Church in Western Canada and the North. Vital Justin Grandin contributed to the written history of the Church in the West, and the author shows great sensitivity to the role played by the bishop in this respect. We penetrate into the inner thoughts of Bishop Grandin about the Hudson's Bay Company and, later, about the Government of Canada, both insensitive to the needs of his native peoples.

This, however, is but one small aspect of the book. Frank Dolphin, through the life of Grandin, invites the reader to accompany the missionary through numerous adventures, both physical and spiritual, thus allowing for a better understanding of the deep faith and dedication of this humble Oblate of Mary Immaculate. If, at times, the reader is struck by the enormity of the task facing Vital Grandin, he is much more amazed by the results obtained. God indeed chooses the humble of this world to accomplish great things !

Under Frank Dolphin's pen, truth is indeed stranger than fiction. Yet the author invented nothing. He simply tells the story as it is — a beautiful story, filled with a humble man's total faith in God's will and always willing to accept the crosses he had to bear, even if he thought himself unworthy of the great responsibilities thrust upon him.

When Vital Grandin arrived at Saint Boniface in 1854, there were only five Catholic missionaries to serve all of Western Canada and the North. Upon his death in 1902, he left sixty-five well-organized missions, fifty schools, three hospitals and two seminaries, and a reputation for holiness that more than half a century has not erased among those who have read accounts of his life.

Reader, beware. Vital Grandin is much alive in Frank Dolphin's book, and you cannot read it without being deeply moved.

Roger G. MOTUT, CM, PhD,
Emeritus Professor of Languages
University of Alberta

Preface

Bishop Vital Justin Grandin, the "Indian bishop" of Western Canada, travelled more than 25,000 miles on snowshoes from one isolated mission to another and countless other miles by dogsled and horseback. These facts give some indication of the devotion this French missionary bishop had to the Church and to the Indians and Metis. Ready to sacrifice his own life at any time for the sake of his people, he came close to death several times, twice in less than a month on the ice of Great Slave Lake.

Vital Justin Grandin (1829–1902), a member of the Oblate Missionaries of Mary Immaculate and the first bishop of St. Albert, later the archdiocese of Edmonton, never considered himself fit to lead the young Church in the West. His health was poor from childhood, forcing him to spend weeks and months in bed, and he had a speech impediment.

His friends called him the "Indian bishop" because he was such an advocate for native peoples in the councils of the whites. He saw himself as a bent reed pointing toward the cross — the symbol he chose for his episcopal coat of arms, which carried the motto Infirma mundi elegit Deus — "God chooses the weak of the world." This missionary bishop of the nineteenth century can teach much about the qualities of loyalty, patience and understanding, qualities needed in every age.

This book is not meant to be a scholar's treatment of Grandin's life, but rather a sketch of the man and his adventures in the early days of the settlement of the Northwest. I have drawn heavily on the works of three French Oblate writers for the rich experiences of Grandin's life: Émile Jonquet, O.M.I., Mgr Grandin (Montreal: 1903); Léon Hermant, O.M.I., Le serviteur de Dieu, Vital Justin Grandin (Bruxelles: Messager de Marie Immaculée, 1937; published in English as Thy Cross My Stay: The Life of the Servant of God Vital Justin Grandin [Toronto: The Mission Press, 1948]); and Paul-Émile Breton, O.M.I., Vital Grandin, O.M.I.: la merveilleuse aventure de "l'évêque sauvage" des Prairies et du Grand Nord (Paris: A. Fayard, 1960).

I am indebted to these writers and to many other people. In particular, I wish to thank Dr. Roger Motut of the University of Alberta for his translation work and encouragement; Father Tony Duhaime, O.M.I., who first suggested writing Grandin's story, and the members of his committee for Oblate causes; Mr. Guy Lacombe, chairman of the committee; and Nicole Clériot, who translated Jonquet's book for me.

I would like to dedicate this book to the memory of all Oblate missionaries, as well as to those in the present, and those priests and brothers still to take up Grandin's work.

1

Burning Ice

HE MAN cradled the youth in his arms, waiting for death. The wind tore at the cariboo hide wrapped around the shivering figures, threatening to rip away the blankets that sheltered the two from the blizzard. The sled dogs, set free from their harness, burrowed into the thin snow cover of Great Slave Lake, looking for a resting place after ten hours of dodging tree stumps and jagged chunks of ice. The fine snowflakes driven by the biting wind erased all signs of the trail to St. Joseph's Mission at Fort Resolution, a warm haven from the storm only a few miles away. Even the dogs, those wary navigators, could not find the trail on this violent December night in 1863.

The man jerked his head to check the blankets billowing in the wind. He lunged as one broke loose from the upright snowshoes and flapped in warning. The wind beat on his forehead. A hundred needles stabbed at the exposed skin.

The two, Vital Grandin, a Roman Catholic bishop, and Jean-Baptiste Pépin, a young Metis, had fallen behind their companions who had rushed ahead to bring the happy news to the isolated mission that the bishop was on his way.

"The Great Spirit has smiled on us with fine weather. We will tell the priests so they can be ready." Then they were gone.

The weather quickly changed once the guides were beyond shouting distance. The clear blue sky turned a flat grey. The wind moaned softly, like a friend urging them on, caressing one moment ; the next, taunting the two to find cover on the icy desert.

Grandin quickly recognized the danger. The snow swirled around them, making zigzag patterns which blocked out the trail and confused the dogs. He stopped to search the sky for some sign of a break in the storm, praying fervently for God's help. The bishop realized the storm would not clear, only grow more fierce. He had faced danger in the huge mission territory before. On each occasion he confidently placed his safety in God's hands. If God wanted him to survive, then he would. If the Master demanded the sacrifice of his life, he was ready to offer it. But surely God did not demand the boy's young life ?

Should they push on and exhaust what energy they and the dogs had left ? Or was it better to make a shelter and wait out the storm ? For the moment they huddled in the sled, the cold biting deeply, the numbness touching their bones. The terrified Baptiste began to cry, the tears freezing to his cheeks. Grandin tried singing, then he prayed to calm the youth. How long before they froze to death ?

"Bless me, Father." Baptiste started his final confession. Grandin put his ear to the quivering mouth. Between the sobs he listened to a litany of minor faults only a fifteen-year-old would consider serious enough to keep him from the Great Spirit, his friend the bishop often talked about.

"Ego te absolvo in nomine Patris... I absolve you from your sins, in the name of the Father..." How strange the Latin words sounded, how foreign, out of place in the frigid wilderness. Yet how beautiful and consoling for two people facing death, helpless and alone. If only he had someone to whom he could confess his sins. He was ready to sacrifice his life without a word of complaint or hesitation. Grandin had arrived in St. Boniface, August 14, 1854, from France to bring the message of God's salvation to the Indians. When that was done, he wanted a martyr's death, but that would be a long way off. The Roman Catholic Oblate Missionaries of Mary Immaculate had only begun their work to bring Christianity to Northwest Canada. How could Grandin give in to death without a struggle? God wanted him to fight for life.

Ah, a bowl of hot soup, how good it would taste! After searching his empty provision bag one last time, he decided to struggle on toward the mission in the hope a search party would double back to rescue them. The journey was painful. Grandin cried out every time his injured toe struck a piece of ice. Then new danger confronted them. He noticed Baptiste falling asleep. Grandin tried everything, shaking the youth, singing, praying, to keep him alert. Just ahead in the dim light was the answer, a deep snowdrift. He dug a hole, spread out the blankets and put the youth into the freezing bed. But how could he stop the wind from stealing their blankets? The bishop led the dogs to the corners of the blankets which they anchored by digging into the drift. Then he piled snow over the youth and lay down beside him.

He felt his damp clothes stiffen as the perspiration from his heavy work began to freeze. When the moisture turned to ice, there was no place to warm his hands. The two travellers wanted desperately to sleep, but if they dared to close their eyes they might never wake up. They spent the long fitful hours tossing, turning, blowing on their hands. Suddenly Grandin jumped to his feet. In the narrow threads of dawn he spotted land.

"Baptiste! Get up, quickly. I see land. The Great Spirit has saved us." The youth burst through the drift in a shower of snow.

"I see it. I see it."

Land meant wood, the crackle of flames, the soothing warmth of the fire. Grandin quickly packed their gear and in the bottom of his bag found some tea. Already he savored each steaming sip. There was another reason to hurry. One of his heels had lost almost all sensation; it was freezing. Baptiste felt a tingling in his own heels. For both of them to put on snowshoes was too painful. They must break the drifts without them.

Hand in hand they fought their way, slipping and sliding. Were they victims of a mirage? The land was so close but always just beyond their footsteps. They lowered their heads to break the wind. Grandin stubbed his sore toe again. This time he yelled with joy for he saw a dead tree. Land at last.

Baptiste ran ahead to gather some twigs. The promise of warmth gave him new energy. They coaxed slivers of bark to burn. The tiny flames flickered and grew until snow in the pot turned into inky tea. As they blew and sipped the warm drink, they noticed the snarling wind was again like yesterday's whisper. The sky grew pink, then a deep red, like the glow from the potbelly stove at St. Joseph's Mission. Last night's storm had blown itself out.

Ice crystals glistened in the cold air. Nature's calm relieved Grandin's anxiety. Thanking God for leading them out of danger to the refuge of the pine grove, he scanned the horizon for a familiar landmark. He let out another whoop.

"Look, there on the lake. Two abandoned sleds. We are near the mission. God has saved us."

With rescue in sight the two laughed and cried, shouted and danced in a torrent of emotion. Gone was their resignation to death, the two survivors were happy to be alive. Another reason to rejoice — the sleds were the ones which had gone ahead. Baptiste's father and uncle had risked their lives to search for them. They had carried flaming torches and shouted Grandin's and Baptiste's names, but the wind had muffled their cries.

The bishop and the youth packed their blankets and quickly hitched the yapping dogs. Within fifteen minutes they spotted the mission house. Smoke curled from the chimney, but there was no sign of anyone.

Grandin pushed against the chapel door, stopping at the sound of Father Émile Petitot's voice across the tiny room. The black vestments signalled a Mass for the dead. Of course, the missionary was offering a Mass for the repose of the souls of the two lost travellers. He looked up from the altar to see the bishop standing beside him, face wreathed in hoarfrost. Petitot grabbed the edge of the altar to steady himself. The dead were alive — thanks to be God. The two men embraced joyfully. There was so much they wanted to say but words would not come. The emotional meeting was almost too much for the priest to finish what now became a Mass of thanksgiving. Grandin also celebrated Mass to thank God for what those who knew the dangers of winter travel believed to be a miraculous escape.

The bishop spent the rest of the day describing the details of the adventure on the ice which had almost cost them their lives. Fathers Petitot and Zéphyrin Gascon relived every moment with Grandin so vividly the three burst into tears several times as the tension broke. The priests told of their search far into the night, firing their rifles in a desperate attempt to make contact. Now they thanked and praised God for his mercy in saving Grandin and Baptiste. For the missionaries, the experience invigorated their lives.

"Stay with us to celebrate Christmas." Grandin agreed but as soon as the feast was over he planned to leave for Providence Mission. Hardly had he recovered from one confrontation with death than he was ready to face more danger to visit his priests and the people who lived in scattered bands. His heroics were not unique, but only the missionaries shared his motives. Other men criss-crossed the wilderness. Indians, Metis, explorers, fur traders travelled the rivers and lakes by canoe in spring and summer. Once the waterways froze, dog teams and snowshoes carried them to their remote destinations. Explorers and fur traders also suffered cold, hunger and loneliness. For them, the prize was an easier route or a rich harvest of furs to sell in Europe.

Grandin and his Oblates had none of these triumphs to sustain their sufferings and privation. By his own admission, it was the example of traders and others that forced the missionaries to gamble their lives gladly. What the missionaries did have was a deeply rooted desire to spread the good news of the Gospel. For them, it was a prize far more valuable than any load of furs.

Grandin wrote in his diary, "Oh, how painful it is in this vast country with which I am entrusted. Not a single pelt is lost, but souls that cost the blood of Jesus Christ are lost every day. Would I hesitate to sacrifice myself? Never."

The two priests at St. Joseph's were not surprised to see the bishop checking the sky and wind as soon as Christmas was over. With the right weather, he could return to Providence Mission across treacherous Great Slave Lake. Although he was daring, he was not reckless. The escape from the earlier storm was warning enough to prepare well for the trip in the coldest month of the year.

Once again Baptiste walked at the bishop's side along with his father and another guide. Six of their strongest dogs strained to pull the sled, loaded with enough provisions for the trip that would take six days or more. The weather held, offering sunny days and clear nights when the campfire smoke climbed in a column through the moonlight. After a hot evening meal, the four talked and prayed, thanking God for another day of safe travel. Then they planned the next day, discussing the route and landmarks to guide their way to Providence.

Trusting his guide's apparent knowledge of the terrain, Grandin failed to notice his growing nervousness. The guide stopped often to check the trail and peer at the horizon. Finally, after two days of this routine, the bishop asked, "What's wrong?"

"I am afraid we are lost. Everything looks the same."

Grandin remained silent. He looked at the endless ice and snowdrifts stretching to the horizon. They decided to spend the rest of the day searching for a way out of the white maze. In the distance they spotted what they thought were islands in the frozen lake. Should they know these landmarks? Perhaps nature was misleading them but they couldn't take a chance. Baptiste's father urged the dogs to race ahead to the islands but like blocks controlled by a hidden magician the islands were always just beyond their reach. Finally, the islands cruelly faded from the travellers' sight. Their faces reflected the crushing disappointment when they realized they had been chasing a mirage. The good Lord was certainly testing Grandin's faith and confidence. The old year was all but gone ; the new one offered little. There was hardly any food left to celebrate the new year's arrival.

They ate the last of their provisions in silence. Gone was the singing and joking that usually ended the day. To thank God for watching over the travellers would be difficult. How could Grandin inspire his companions to love God when they were teetering on the brink of death ? Even the bishop struggled to accept the will of God who was asking his missionary and the boy to face death on the trail for the second time in only three weeks. Praying that God would provide a safe passage through the ice and snow they tried to sleep before facing another terrifying day. When they awoke, the party made a decision about their survival. Unless they found their way the next day, they must start boiling pieces of cariboo hide. The next step would be to kill and eat the dogs.

They spent New Year's Eve searching for a trail that would lead them to Providence, hot food and a warm bed. After wandering on the ice during the brief daylight hours, they made camp. Frustration and disappointment welled up inside them. The spit and snap of the burning wood provided some comfort but there was no food for hungry stomachs. The travellers covered themselves with snow, wondering what, if anything, the new year would bring.

"Pray for us, Bishop. The good God will listen to you."

After a fitful night the three men and the youth broke camp. Hunger gnawed at their stomachs. Before taking off they searched for animal tracks, hoping to kill a deer or even a rabbit, anything to give them something to eat. The barking of the famished dogs underlined their desperation. The travellers knelt to say the rosary before facing another day of wandering on the ice. When the last Hail Mary was finished, Grandin decided to wait alone while the others searched for a way out of the snowy labyrinth. He had a sacred duty to perform. He wanted to renew his religious profession, the vows solemnly pledged eleven years before.

He took his missionary cross, the cross he had received on the day he fully embraced the religious life as an Oblate of

Mary Immaculate, and knelt on the ice holding the cross firmly before him. His eyes were closed tightly, shutting out the waves of fear and desperation that engulfed him. He was a student once again in France, in Marseilles. There was Bishop Charles Eugène de Mazenod, the founder of the Oblates and his friend, the one who had inspired and now sustained Grandin's work among the Indians and Metis.

"In the name of Our Lord Jesus Christ... I, Vital Justin Grandin, promise to God and vow poverty, chastity and obedience for life. I also swear and vow perseverance for life..."

He opened his eyes, expecting to see his brother Oblates gathered around him. He realized how alone he was, one man, kneeling not before his founder but before the grandeur of God's creation. The glare of the sun on the pure white snow temporarily blinded him.

"My God, I offer you my life, if that is your will. But I pray that you will allow me to serve you, no matter what the sacrifice, for as long as I am able." He regularly made the same offer to God on his travels.

As he squinted over the lake, the mysterious islands beckoned. Should they spend another day searching for the trail or retrace the long trek to St. Joseph's Mission? "That means killing and eating the dogs, one by one. I can't do that. Well, only if we are starving."

When the others returned, Grandin told them to cheer up. After all, he and Baptiste had survived the blizzard on the lake only a few weeks before. God hadn't abandoned them when death had threatened and wouldn't now. "One more day of searching," Grandin said, "then I've got something else to suggest."

The mirages appeared and disappeared, taunting them, beckoning the hungry travellers to turn one way, then another. By three the sun slipped below the horizon, time to make camp. After another night of tossing and turning on an empty stomach, Bishop Grandin explained his plan to his anxious companions.

"First, let's pray. We'll tell God we are like the wise men from the East, searching for the Christ Child. They were guided by a star. If God will show us the way to Providence, then we will celebrate a High Mass there on the feast of the Epiphany. That's only four days away."

As the four broke camp and moved off, the mirages shimmered in the crisp air. The bishop noticed one patch of land looked different from the others. For some reason it didn't fade from view like the other phantoms. He studied it carefully, afraid to get his hopes too high. "I think I recognize that point," he told Baptiste's father. "It's solid ground. That's not one of nature's tricks."

The guide shouted at the dogs and turned the sled so sharply he almost turned it over in the rush to reach the point. Finally, there in the snow they spotted sled tracks. The four whooped for joy, just as Grandin and Baptiste had done on the day they discovered the sleds after their night of terror. The dogs broke into a run. They could taste the raw meat waiting for them. The northern wanderers beat Epiphany's wise men by a few hours.

These incidents in the early years of the missionary bishop show how God fashions strength out of weakness. Just as Grandin as a youth had overcome physical weakness, a speech impediment, poverty and rejection by Church officials, he now overcame storms, hardships and loneliness to serve his scattered missions in Western Canada.

"What a splendid bishop you have there in North America," French journalist Louis Veuillot would write. "He has shown me the truth of the saying that ice burns."

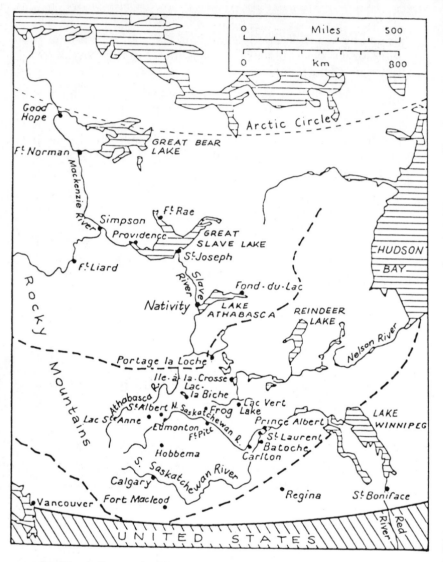

St. Albert diocese in 1871. (Adapted from P. E. Breton, *Vital Grandin, O.M.I.* [Paris: A. Fayard, 1960]).

Vital Grandin as a young bishop. (Courtesy Archives Deschâtelets, Ottawa)

Bishop Grandin in middle age. (Courtesy Archives Deschâtelets, Ottawa)

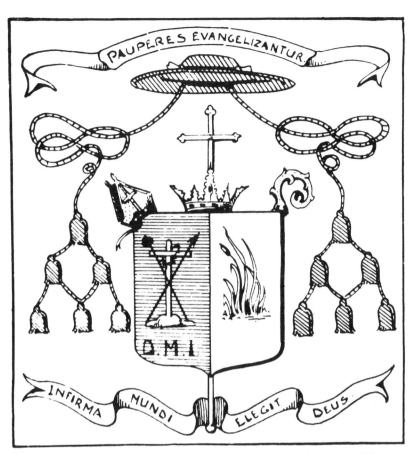

Grandin's episcopal coat of arms. The bent reed points toward the cross. Underneath the cross are the initials O.M.I., the abbreviation for the Oblates of Mary Immaculate. To the top, the Oblate motto, *Pauperes evangelizantur,* "The poor have the good news preached to them" (Matt. 11:5); at the bottom, Grandin's episcopal motto, *Infirma mundi elegit Deus,* "God chooses the weak of the world" (1 Cor. 1:27-28). (Courtesy Archives Deschâtelets, Ottawa)

St. Albert's first cathedral. Constructed in 1861 of logs, this 30 by 25 foot cabin served as a chapel and residence for Father Lacombe. With the 1868 appointment of Grandin as bishop it became the diocese's first cathedral. It was replaced in 1870 by a church which accommodated 400 people. (Courtesy Archives Deschâtelets, Ottawa)

Bishop's residence, built 1882-87. Grandin's residence later became the parish rectory. Declared an historical site in 1977, it was restored 1981-82. (Original drawing by Cheryl Ray, 1982)

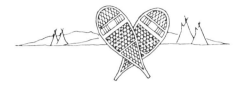

2

The Struggle Begins

LONG before young Vital Justin Grandin had heard of Northwest Canada and its native peoples, an interest in the priesthood awakened in him. The four-year-old boy growing up in 1833 imitated anyone who made a strong impression on him. The assistant priest in his family's parish at Aron, a small village in the north of France, became his model. The young priest often visited the Grandin home. The nine living brothers and sisters in the family of thirteen children laughed at his stories and sang along with him, often making up their own songs.

Marie and Jean Grandin proudly told the story about the day the priest first asked Vital the question so many adults put to children, "What are you going to be when you grow up?" The young boy tightly held his mother's hand and hid in the folds of her skirt. The priest bent down close to the child, wondering what he would say. Vital tried to hide his face.

"I want to be like my brother Jean," he whispered. "Jean studies at the parish. He is learning to be a priest. I want to make miracles."

"Come on, then, a priest has to give sermons. Let's hear yours."

Vital climbed on a chair. He had one sermon, the one the priest had taught him. "I am only a little boy. I can't tell you what the Gospel is for today. I do know whoever raises himself up will be lowered and the person who lowers himself will be raised up. Remember that." The priest and the Grandin family would laugh at Vital's serious expression.

Marie remembered the day Vital made his First Communion. He was not quite ten years old, young for that time. Even as an old man he would not forget that memorable day. He would celebrate its anniversary faithfully each year for the rest of his life. Vital told his mother the desire to be a priest welled up in him as he approached the altar rail for the first time. In the midst of his joy at receiving the Eucharist, a sudden sadness swept over him. He feared he would never become a priest because his parents were so poor. Even as a small boy he realized how much his parents had to struggle to raise their family. Jean, his eldest brother, had already left for the minor seminary to begin the long years of study leading to the priesthood. Vital remembered the tension in the home when Jean first told their father he wanted to be a priest.

Marie had tried to keep the children quiet while father and son discussed Jean's reasons for choosing the priesthood. His father questioned his son's motives, showing little apparent enthusiasm for his decision. As Marie put her finger to her lips in a sign to make less noise, the children cowered as their father's voice grew louder.

"Jean, you are not good enough to think of becoming a priest. A priest must be a saint. I would rather see you die as a simple farmer than see you turn into a useless priest, one that does a lot of harm."

Marie knew the discussion had made a deep impression on Vital. If his father did not think Jean was good enough to be a priest, then how could Vital ever consider the idea?

Finally, when Jean and his father walked arm in arm into the kitchen to announce the decision — Jean would go to the minor seminary — Marie and the children had laughed and hugged the boy. The parents realized what price must be paid to have a priest in the family. They would have to work even harder, although they were confident God would provide. To ease the burden, Marie packed Vital's few clothes, kissed him gently on both cheeks and sent him to live with his uncle Michel Patry, who was also his godfather. Vital could earn his keep as a shepherd and would later be joined by his younger sister Mélanie.

"Ah, Vital. Welcome, my boy. Come into your new home. Remember, you are one of the family, not just another one of our shepherds."

Uncle Michel ruffled the eleven-year-old's hair. It would take time for Vital to feel at home with his godfather. But it helped to realize that he was lifting some of the burden from his parents' shoulders. Anyway, he liked the outdoors and was determined to like his new home.

"Mmmm. Smell that fresh air. Look at those sheep. We are going to be friends," the boy told himself bravely.

He got up early each morning to do farm chores, at least those his delicate health would allow. By evening he was tired and went to bed soon after supper. Some nights he cried himself to sleep, just like any young boy cut off from the security of his family. As the months passed there were fewer tears. Uncle Michel spoke to him often about his family. While he admired Vital's mother and father, he disagreed with their approach to life, an approach he felt was not properly preparing the boy for the hard realities of the nineteenth century.

"Your father has made all the wrong moves," he told Vital. "He had a rich farm. Sure, a storm blew down his buildings and washed away his house. But he could have rebuilt them."

The boy sat quietly, afraid to interrupt. Uncle Michel seemed to be blaming his father for the family's poverty. Surely he did only what he thought was God's will for the family? To attack his father was unfair when he was not there to defend himself.

"Then he bought the Pelican, that inn at St. Pierre-la-Cour on the road to Le Mans. That's the place you were born." Michel pointed a finger at Vital. The boy tried to look away but that wagging finger chased his eyes. "Why couldn't he just serve his customers? Oh no, he had to butt into their lives, cutting them off when they had too much to drink. That, my boy, was bad for business. And the Church. Your mother and father spent far too much time praying. They turned you into choirboys, even worse, little priests."

The sudden attack on his family stunned Vital. What was wrong with wanting to follow Jesus' words? To be a priest? If only he could be a priest. He ran from the room with his uncle's words racing after him.

"Prayer and poverty, remember they go together, my little one."

Soon after the incident a letter arrived. "Dear Vital, it is time to return home." When he stepped through the door, there had been a torrent of hugs and questions, "What was it like living with Uncle Michel? We missed you so much. Look how he has grown."

Vital had trouble sleeping that first night at home. He tossed and turned in his old bed. The excitement of the last two years raced through his mind. Only now did he fully realize the extent of his parents' poverty. The realization had dimmed during his stay at Montreuil with his uncle. Now it hit him with the cutting edge of the bitter north wind that blew across the French fields in winter. Compared with his uncle's well-furnished home, his parents had little more than one could find in a monk's cell. His eyes darted across the almost empty room. For a moment he felt sad and uneasy. Then the memory of his family's welcome flooded his mind. How could he be sad? He had his sisters, Rose, Anne and, best of all, Mélanie, his favorite. With her he could at least share his feelings, his desire to be a priest. But how could he tell his parents? Surely his mother would understand.

Vital picked what he thought would be the right moment. Marie was sitting in her favorite chair, quietly humming as she sewed patches on the children's clothes. She glanced at her thirteen-year-old son pacing up and down the large French kitchen. Marie knew Vital wanted to talk but he was afraid to tell her what was bothering him. "Sit down beside me. You're like a big cat prowling up and down."

Her invitation broke the tension. He grinned and ran to his mother's side. He could always depend on her to put him at ease. Marie put her arm around his shoulders and pulled him gently toward her. She looked deeply into his eyes, framed by a thin face and a high forehead. In 1842 Vital suffered from illnesses for which there was no quick cure. A lisp added to his problems. Despite all the obstacles, she knew his desire to be a priest would not die.

Marie's reassurance helped Vital but it did not drive away all his doubts. Perhaps there had been a hint of truth in Uncle Michel's harsh assessment of his parents' attitude toward life. They were willing to sacrifice everything to live by their Christian values. Where did that leave him? Vital pondered his own future as he walked the roads and fields near his home. He could read, a little. His brother Jean had taught him before leaving for the seminary. But he couldn't write. He could never become a priest or anyone much more than a shepherd, unless he found a way to get an education. If the priesthood was beyond him, then he would answer the next best calling. He would become a brother.

A broad smile broke across Jean's face as he listened to Vital. He could sense the pain his brother had suffered in trying to make a decision about his future. Jean shared the anguish Vital felt over his parents' devastating poverty. The older youth realized far better than his brothers and sisters just how hard their parents must work for him to become a priest. Vital thought he had found a way out. When he told Jean his decision, his brother gave him a bear hug. To make the first step easier, he would introduce Vital to the superior of the Brothers of St. Joseph in Le Mans.

Vital's father and mother were pleased. They had talked often about their son's future. His long periods of silence and depression worried them. Now they could celebrate. They stretched their resources enough to find the clothing and other necessities he would need to begin a new life as a brother.

The joy of discovering his future was short-lived. He looked older than fourteen. The director of the juniorate thought Vital was at least sixteen. As a result, the director expected much more from this timid boy who only now was beginning to assert himself after such a sheltered life. The St. Joseph Brothers wanted strong boys, not sickly ones like Vital who suffered from chronic ailments. He was a bad risk. Within three months the superior called him to his office. "I am sure you understand that God's call is not always a clear one. We must sift and study the signs. I am afraid I must tell you that your health does not make you a suitable candidate for a Brother of St. Joseph. I believe you should look somewhere else for your vocation. For that reason I must ask you to leave."

The director's words inflicted a new wound on the sensitive youth. If the brothers didn't want him, where could he turn ? Perhaps he should follow his older brother Frédéric and look for work in Paris. At least he would not be a burden on his parents.

"My dear brother Vital, Paris is not the place for you," Frédéric wrote in reply to Vital's request for help to find a job. "I doubt we could find work to suit your delicate health and your desires."

While the letter struck a further blow at Vital's dream, it contained some understanding of his problem. Frédéric realized his younger, less experienced brother was simply running from his problem. "Keep up your studies while you have the chance. I know life is difficult for you. But you are still so young. Believe me, Paris is not the place for you."

Frédéric had written another letter which his parents read and discussed carefully. They had long known Vital wanted to be a priest. What they had not realized was the frustration and suffering he felt from seeing his goal continually denied. His mother could not put aside Frédéric's plea, "Do something. Vital is getting desperate."

Marie waited for the right moment to reopen the subject with Vital. "Have you given up on the priesthood? Is that why you want to go to Paris?"

"Mother, you know I want to be a priest more than anything else. The thought rarely leaves my mind. How can I ask you and father to sacrifice more than you are now? We have so much love but so little money."

"Vital, God has looked after us through the years. No matter what trials he sends us, God always provides the strength to overcome them. Your father and I want you to be a good priest. The money? Let us worry about that."

Marie hugged her son and he kissed her gently on the cheek. She had no idea where to get the money but she had faith. He hardly knew what to say. All his fretting was over, at least for the present. Now he must concentrate on preparing himself for admission to the minor seminary.

In May, 1845, one of the local priests agreed to teach Vital Latin but was transferred to another parish within a few weeks. The latest setback had one good effect: it drew Vital and Jean, who was eight years older, closer together. They now shared the same vocation. Jean was now studying in the seminary and could teach his brother. For once fortune started to run in Vital's favor.

Anne-Marie, a relative who was a lay sister with the Carmelites of Le Mans, offered Vital room and board. With the basics looked after, she provided some extra money for books and other expenses by selling flowers and religious items. While her financial support was crucial, even more important was her introducing him to an influential nun.

Sister Françoise Cormier, a sister of the Perpetual Adoration of Le Mans, opened her heart to Vital. She recognized the potential that lay well hidden beneath the quiet, shy exterior. She liked his determination. Sister Françoise introduced him to Abbé Alexandre-Léopold Sébaux, the bishop's secretary, who took an immediate liking to Vital and offered to teach him for several hours a week. So began a friendship to last a lifetime. Both men would become bishops, Vital in Canada, the abbé of the diocese of Angoulême in France.

Vital's future seemed assured with such good friends. The abbé used his influence to gain approval for Vital to begin his studies for the priesthood. He learned rapidly to make up for the years he had spent in the fields tending sheep when other boys his age were in school. As the weeks slipped by he looked forward to going home for Christmas. His mother was ill with what his father had warned was a fatal disease. Vital prayed God would cure her. If love could make her better, then there was no doubt about his mother's recovery. Jean received several letters from home each week with news of her worsening condition but he decided not to worry Vital and kept the bad news to himself.

Early in December, 1845, Vital went to Jean's room as he did most mornings. Without turning around, Jean ordered him to leave. "I am very busy. Don't come back today. I'll come to see you." Vital couldn't see the tears that streaked his brother's face. Later that day a cousin broke the news. Their mother was dead.

The strong, deep voices of the seminarians singing the Requiem Mass helped to numb the pain and to fill the void left by the loss of their mother. Vital stared at the coffin with the six huge candles flickering in the grey winter light. Would his hopes for the priesthood die with his mother ?

As they walked to the parish cemetery behind the coffin, Vital kept thinking of what Abbé Sébaux had told him about the harsh lesson of death. "The good Lord is preparing you to be a priest. You must learn what suffering is because you will be called to console those who suffer."

Little did Vital realize he would be called to console the abbé in just a few days when the news arrived that his own mother had died. The deaths of the two women would create an unbreakable bond between the two men.

Vital wept when his mother's coffin slowly sank into the ground. Throughout his life his love for her remained strong. Years later as a bishop in Western Canada, he explained what he believed was the meaning of her death in God's plan for him. "When the Lord took her away, he removed the biggest obstacle to my vocation. If my mother had lived, I might not have had the courage to leave her for God."

3

Call from Afar

THE NEWS devastated old Jean Grandin. His wife was dead. Now he must cope with all the problems of his large family growing up in 1850 in the turmoil of a France reeling from the retribution of the guillotine and the march of its armies across Europe. The revolution and Napoleon's wars had awakened a disturbing new spirit in young people, even those in his family. Their loyalty remained strong but they had a streak of independence. Vital, for one, worried him. Old Jean grew more upset with every step his son took along the road to the major seminary in Le Mans.

Jean jumped back as a coach drawn by two huge black horses charged past, narrowly missing him. The driver looked over his shoulder and shook his fist, cursing the old man for walking directly into the path of his horses. Jean hardly even noticed. Engrossed in Vital's latest desire to do something heroic with his life, the old man hardly knew what was happening around him. Everyone else knew Vital was different but what was he trying to prove? Why couldn't he be satisfied with simply becoming a priest? Hadn't he and Vital's dead mother gone far enough to put the boy's mind at ease? His stubborn son had persisted until they approved of his wish to become a priest. Now Vital was demanding the impossible — not only a priest but a missionary in some faraway land! The sacrifice was too much. Couldn't he be happy in France and serve God just as well here without getting himself killed in a country he knew little about?

Jean rang the bell at the seminary's main entrance. An elderly brother opened the door. He looked at Jean for a moment, then gestured for him to come in. "Monsieur Grandin. Please, please. You want to see Vital. He must be in the garden, trying to study but I think the good weather is too much of a distraction, even for him. Let me call him to the parlor so you can talk."

"Thank you." The old brother always seemed to know what people wanted so there was little need for conversation. Jean watched him disappear down the long hallway, then paced slowly up and down the room with second thoughts engulfing him. Vital had not been much of a burden during the four years he was in the minor seminary at Précigné. Abbé Sébaux had generously provided the money for board and upkeep, even clothing. But this was his son, not Abbé Sébaux's, no matter how devoted the man was to Vital.

"Surely a father has some rights. And a son some responsibility to his family," Jean reassured himself. He couldn't forget the worry caused by Vital's fragile health. Once the rector had called Jean to come quickly because he feared Vital would die. The young student himself had broken the news to the rector in a strange way. He announced he was preparing for two exams.

"First, there is the entrance exam for the major seminary. If I don't take it now, I will worry all summer and ruin my vacation."

"What's the second one, Vital?"

"It's a lot more serious. The doctors have given up all hope for my recovery. I am preparing myself for death. Wouldn't you say it is far more important to prepare for heaven's admission exam than the one for the seminary?"

Vital spent a lot of time in the infirmary. A plaque hung there long after he left, attesting to his stay as a patient. Illness forced him to leave Précigné several times, but always he returned because of his intense desire for the priesthood. Other problems also made life difficult for him. When he arrived at Précigné, he was awkward, shy and, worst of all, poorly educated compared with the other students — the perfect butt for their jokes. Few realized his sensitivity and the hurt he suffered. Even as a young man of eighteen he broke into uncontrollable sobbing when he talked about life at the seminary.

To learn everything he needed had been difficult. But another struggle was tearing at Vital. One student spoke incessantly of the missions, to the point of being a bore. Vital tried to avoid him and his constant talk of sacrificing one's life in the mysterious lands of Asia and Africa. Now Vital also wanted to leave France.

"Father, how good to see you but you look worried."

"Who wouldn't be worried with a son who wants to go halfway round the world and live in some foreign land, even if it is to carry the faith."

"You don't know how frightened I am to become a missionary, father. But something keeps eating at me inside. I fought against it as hard as I could but it wouldn't go away. That's all behind me now."

"What do you mean? You've changed your mind?"

"Not at all. I made up my mind during a retreat. No matter what the cost, I must be a missionary."

"And that cost, must your family pay it as well?"

Vital looked into his father's face. The years of struggle had left their marks on the man he loved so dearly but life had also presented the son with his own set of scars. Uncertainty had been Vital's shepherd, leading him from one thorn bush to another, like the sheep on his godfather's farm. Somehow he must find the words to explain to his father the change he had undergone. "The doubts that plagued me through my studies and sick days at Précigné and Le Mans are finally gone. It is Abbé Sébaux who settled my vocation. Could I, someone with so little talent, could I dare be a missionary? I pleaded with the abbé. He opened his Bible at the First Epistle to the Corinthians and began to read. I discovered the first disciples had to work through the same problem: how can a weak man or woman measure up to the ideals set by Jesus' life? The answer, of course, is they can't.

"I'll never forget what the abbé read. 'The foolish things of the world has God chosen to put to shame the wise, and the weak things of the world has God chosen to put to shame the strong...' That was all I needed to hear. My whole life of poverty, ignorance and weakness made sense at last. My shortcomings would be my strength because God, not I, would be in control from that moment."

Jean was amazed at his son's new confidence but believed Vital still could be persuaded to change his mind and prepare himself for the life of a parish priest near his family. "You have to be smart to be a missionary. And have good health. The trick is survival in those places. The life is hard. Remember all those stories about the natives, how cruel they are to foreigners? Could you take a life of that?"

Vital did not reply. He couldn't argue with his father, especially when he misunderstood the significance of St. Paul's description of God's choice of the weak of the world.

"You know I want you to stay in this country," his father pleaded. He wanted the security of his family around him. Now Marie was gone, he was alone to face the advancing years. Jean had one more argument that might succeed where his others had failed.

"Vital, I have been talking to a priest about your future. A priest who knows about these things. He says you would make a big mistake to spend your life in the foreign missions. My friend says you are well known in the bishop's house. You have a good future as a parish priest here. Take that card and play it."

But Jean soon realized his arguments were useless. Vital had made up his mind to join a missionary group. Nothing he could say or do would change his son's decision. He wanted to study in Paris at the Society of the Foreign Missions, a small missionary group formed in 1663 to work in Asia.

"God's will, Vital. My blessings." The old man turned to leave. Vital put his arms around his father and gently hugged him. He knew the conflict over his vocation was crushing his father. For Vital, it was even more intense yet he remained firm.

"I know how hard it will be to say goodbye, father. But I must go wherever God decides to send me. Everything is in God's hands. It will work out. You'll see." Vital had no real understanding of the pain final parting would bring. Long before he was to leave France behind, he must face even more rejection, disappointments and endless farewells.

Vital boarded a train for Paris with only his brother Jean, now a priest, to see him off. He had decided not to tell his father and sister Mélanie he was leaving in order to spare them the pain of separation. The real reason was he could not bear to say goodbye. Fifty years later, the scene was still vivid in his mind. He wrote in his diary that of all the hardships he had endured, the cold, the hunger, the dirt and the lice, nothing had been more difficult than leaving home. "I was convinced I would meet my family again only in heaven."

As the train puffed and billowed steam in a slow jerking start, Vital pushed through a knot of waving passengers to a window for a final glance. He could see by the expression on Jean's face that his brother was upset by more than Vital's departure. Jean had secretly desired to do the same thing, but with Vital assuming the care of the family to free Jean for the foreign missions. When Vital arrived in Paris, he wrote to Jean in order to soothe his hurt feelings. "How could I forget all you have done to help me prepare for this change in my life ?"

Vital apologized to Mélanie for leaving without seeing her. "I did it to spare you the heartbreak of our separating from each other." To his father he wrote, "It gave me great pleasure to hear from Abbé Sébaux of your courageous sacrifice. Pray often for your poor Vital that I may become a saintly priest."

With his family relationships repaired, Vital Grandin turned to the job of becoming a missionary. September's warm days quickly passed into fall and winter. He felt at ease with his professors' emphasis on the growth of the spiritual life rather than the formal theological training for the priesthood. He regarded the seminary discipline and study much like the training of an elite army corps. The Society of the Foreign Missions was so selective it had grown to only sixty priests in two hundred years and had a reputation as a band of progressive and pious missionaries. The young students thrilled to the stories of the missionary exploits in China, the sacrifices and beatings willingly suffered by the society's priests to establish the Church.

Vital wrote to his family, "Our bursar is the most famous of all... He received so many beatings with a stick that he left his backside in Tonkin. He would have left his life if a French consul hadn't arranged his freedom."

In the hothouse of missionary tales and activity, Grandin's character began to mature. However, he still suffered pangs of loneliness. There was no way he could separate himself completely from his family. His feelings pulled him in opposite directions: total dedication to what he believed was his calling, and love and concern for his family. Later he would learn just how much he needed those strong family ties to sustain the difficult work he would undertake during his life as a priest and bishop.

While it was normal for spiritual directors to advise seminarians to cut family ties and not to look back, his brother Jean knew the interior battle Vital was fighting. "I shall be ever thankful for what you did to make this sacrifice less difficult," the future missionary wrote him. In addition to all the human support, Grandin sought the help of Our Lady of Victories, one of many titles given to the Blessed Virgin. He prayed often at the shrine of the miraculous Madonna in Montmartre, a district of Paris. He wrote to Abbé Sébaux, "I believe I owe my vocation to her. I hope to be faithful to her and to show my gratitude."

Just when Grandin believed his vocation was settled, that he would be accepted by the mission society, the abbé delivered a shocking message, "Your Father Superior asked me to break the news to you. They would like to admit you to the society, but your speech impediment will make it difficult for you to speak the Asian languages."

"Expelled." Grandin repeated the word. "Expelled, just when I thought everything was going so well." He slumped into a chair.

Sébaux tried to console him. "All is not over for your dream to be a missionary. You can knock on other doors. There are other missionary congregations. Of course, there is always the seminary at Le Mans. You would be welcome there and your family, in particular your brother Jean, would rejoice. He still wants to trade places with you."

"I was so happy here. But you know something, Abbé, I am still happy. God wants it this way, I accept his verdict. God be blessed. I will look for another congregation."

The abbé shook his head. Grandin's acceptance and the resolve to overcome yet another rejection showed new strength that was greatly encouraging. Instead of feeling sorry for himself, he took the suggestion of another priest friend who urged him to apply to the Missionary Oblates of Mary Immaculate. Here was a new French congregation, founded in 1816 out of the aftermath of the French Revolution, with missions in Ceylon, South Africa and North America.

Word arrived December 15, 1851, that the Oblate Fathers had accepted him as a novice. What a Christmas present! He had found a new home. Before leaving the mission society, he made the rounds of the priests and seminarians to wish them well for the new year. He promised to pray for their success in the difficult and often dangerous work in foreign lands. Many of them could not understand the superior's decision to reject Grandin as a missionary. Everything had seemed right about Vital, despite his speech impediment.

With only forty-four francs in his wallet, Grandin faced travelling to the Oblate novitiate near Vinay in Isère, a remote part of southern France. To pay the travel costs, he sold some of his clothes. Even with enough money there was no guarantee he would get there. France was in another state of political upheaval. The popular Louis Napoleon, Napoleon III, had hung on to the president's office through a December 2, 1851, coup d'état just two weeks before Grandin left Paris for the novitiate.

Grandin boarded a night train, travelling south through central France where the army was mopping up pockets of resistance. He pressed his eyes to the window, trying to see something in the dark by framing his face with his hands. He worried about the repeated rumors of barricades, shootings and the arrest of anyone who opposed the coup, but he saw nothing more than sleeping towns as the train chugged through the black countryside. In the morning he and the other passengers boarded a boat at Châlons for the rest of the trip down the Saône River to Lyon. Fog and choppy water tossed them around so much that some passengers became sick.

Ding. Ding. Ding. The ship's bell sounded a warning. Grandin heard someone shout, "My God, we're going to crash." The ship veered sharply in the heavy fog, narrowly missing an unseen obstacle. Long before their journey was due to end the ship docked in a remote spot. Without any explanation the captain ordered the passengers off the boat. As they streamed down the gangplank, an angry murmur grew into shouts. Passengers demanded an explanation from the crew who simply shrugged and continued unloading the baggage and freight. " What's going on ? We're seven hours at least from Lyon. And you dump us here. Where will we spend the night ?" Finally the captain gave a hint of the danger the passengers faced.

"It's the coup. It's not wise to travel on the river at night. You must stay here. Then tomorrow, well, we'll see what happens."

The two hundred people milled about at the side of the ship, searching for their luggage in the dark. Local men walked through the crowd, offering for a stiff fee to carry the bags and boxes to a small hotel. "You can spend the night there. Coaches will take you to Lyon tomorrow," they told the angry passengers in an attempt to calm them.

Grandin was tired and upset. He had carefully budgeted for the trip. Now it would cost him more precious francs to get to the novitiate. He followed the passengers to the village of Ville Franche where they spent the night. The unfairness of having to pay an extra fare made him forget his usual shyness. When it came time to negotiate the coach fare, Vital argued so vigorously that the coach drivers finally settled for thirteen francs a passenger, a lot of money at that.

"At last," Grandin said to a man standing next to him. The horses looked anxious to start the trip, nervously prancing and snorting, trying to break loose from the stable boy's grasp.

"Look out," the driver yelled as Grandin hoisted his trunk into the rack. The boy let go as the horses bolted, throwing the men backwards. The trunk came crashing to the ground, narrowly missing its owner and the driver, and it split open, strewing clothes and personal effects on the wet ground.

Some of the passengers laughed at the sight of the things strewn on the ground. The mishap not only broke the trunk but also the tension. Grandin's face grew red until he saw the humor and sighed with relief. He hurriedly picked up his clothes and belongings. Soon they were in the coach and the horses broke into a trot. "Surely nothing else can happen," he whispered as he watched the trees drift past in a swirl of fog.

Charles Joseph Eugène de Mazenod, 1782-1861. In 1826 the Vatican approved Eugène de Mazenod's establishment of the Oblates of Mary Immaculate; in 1837 the founder of the missionary institute became bishop of Marseilles. He was declared blessed in 1975. (Courtesy Archives Deschâtelets, Ottawa)

4

Into the Unknown

"**S**TOP, EVERYONE. Stop for a minute. Can you hear that sound?" The priest leading the group of novices cupped his hand to his ear. Far in the distance they heard a faint call echoing through the valley.

"Olee, olee, olee..."

Grandin recognized the sound immediately. "I know what that is. That's a shepherd calling to his flock," he told the other young men perched on rocks jutting from the mountain-side.

"How do you know?" they demanded.

"How do I know?" Grandin laughed, "Believe it or not, I was a shepherd once, when I was just a small boy."

Memories flooded his mind of times spent with his sister Mélanie, tending the sheep. He could still feel the rough linen shirt, oversized pants passed down from his brothers, and the wooden shoes for plodding through the mud. Now he listened to the soothing voice of another young shepherd, the notes hanging like crystals in the clear mountain air.

"We should answer him so he knows he's not alone," Grandin suggested. The others tried to imitate the anonymous shepherd. What they produced in enthusiasm and volume they lost in quality. Finally they ended their jarring attempts with a laugh and continued the climb.

Grandin amazed himself not with his singing but with his newly found stamina. Here he was dodging boulders, tramping through water and slush, with only black bread to eat, a foretaste of the hardships he would face as a missionary in Northwest Canada. Since his arrival at the novitiate of the Oblates of Mary Immaculate, the one thing he feared most was a new bout of illness which would force his superiors to conclude he didn't have the strength to undergo the rigors of missionary life. That fear tortured him most on days when the master of novices issued the order, "Don't go for a walk this afternoon. I want you to take a brother to Vinay. He is leaving the novitiate." The very thought that one day he might be that brother terrified Grandin. He would never forget the shock of having to leave the Foreign Missions seminary in Paris. He felt some of the crushing hurt of those who must resume the search for their vocation.

Despite all his fears about health, Grandin marvelled at his growing strength. He was now surviving tough mountain hikes which two years before would have put him on his back for weeks. He found new spiritual strength as well. Living in the shadow of his illnesses caused enough anxiety, but even more of a constant worry was the attitude of his family. His sudden departure for the Oblate novitiate, again without a proper farewell, had left his brothers upset and angry. Instead of ignoring their protests with the excuse that he had his own life to live, Grandin wrote long letters trying to understand and defuse their hostility.

"I was both very pleased with your letters and very hurt," he wrote. "Very pleased, because I recognized your kind-heartedness in those letters bathed in your tears. I cannot express how very happy I was to hear about the news of your generosity toward the good Lord.

"I was very hurt because you did not dare to tell me about your anguish and confusion. Why would you not write to me when you have sad news to break to me? I am happy to know that too. Indeed, the good Lord likes our family since he allows us to share in his suffering."

Grandin's openness restored his family's confidence and support. His brother Florent, who had showed the most hostility, eventually encouraged three of his sons to dedicate their lives to the Church. With his health under control, at least for the present, and the attitude of his family improving, Grandin now wondered where he would spend his life as an Oblate missionary. The answer came one day during a recreation break. He saw a group of novices gathered around a young priest in the novitiate garden. With him were two of Vital's old friends from Précigné, Father René Rémas and Father Valentin Végreville, both Oblates.

"Who is the priest?" Grandin whispered to one of his confreres as he moved closer to the center of the circle.

"Don't you know? He is Bishop Alexandre Taché from Canada."

"A bishop! He hardly looks old enough."

"He is young. Just twenty-eight. I guess you have to be young and tough to survive in that country. No place for old worn-out clerics. He's looking for priests to work with him in his diocese."

Grandin could feel his pulse beat faster. His two friends suddenly recognized him. "How good to see a friendly face from home. Come and meet Bishop Taché."

He dropped to one knee to kiss the bishop's ring in the customary way. Taché held out one hand, placing the other on Grandin's shoulder. "Brother Vital, you know these two priests. They are coming to Canada with me to work among the Indians. Why don't you come too when you finish your seminary studies? We have plenty of room for you." They all laughed when they thought of the size of Bishop Taché's St. Boniface diocese which covered most of Northwestern Canada, an area as large as Europe.

Grandin searched the bishop's face, then sighed with relief. "Thank you for the invitation. I was worried about learning the languages. Yes! Yes! I will come right after my ordination."

Taché and the two priests left but the impact of their visit remained strong. Vital viewed his promise to join them in Canada as a solemn commitment, one to inspire his whole life as an Oblate. With that objective firmly fixed in his mind, he used the remaining months of his year in the novitiate to prepare for the critical step of promising life-long poverty, chastity, obedience and perseverance to his superiors and to God.

He wrote to his brother Jean, "It is definitely the meaning of the cross which will be put around my neck to remind me, every minute, that the life of an Oblate is one of self-sacrifice and a continual offering... Until now, our congregation has lacked martyrs. I wish I could be blessed with being the first Oblate martyr. What a joy for me and an honor for you, my brother."

As January 1, 1853, approached, the joyful day Grandin was to make his solemn profession, he began to worry. Despite his conviction that God and Our Lady of Victories had led him to the novitiate, was he giving himself without compromise to the religious life? These conflicting forces — the desire to sacrifice himself, his fear of rejection, and the bond that tied him so securely to his family — fought a final winner-take-all battle during the days of silence and meditation in preparation for his solemn profession.

New Year's Day finally arrived. Grandin stood nervously in the novitiate chapel, eager to make his promises and to receive his crucifix, a precious gift for life. His hands fingered the brass figure on the wooden cross. His voice trembled as he repeated the vows making him an Oblate.

"I was emotionally upset, drunk with happiness... Once I had become an Oblate, I considered myself married. I have never wanted to take back what I had given." Grandin's commitment and his formal acceptance by the congregation freed him of the fears that had caused so much turmoil in his life.

"Bon voyage, bon voyage, Frère Vital," the priests and novices shouted three days later when he climbed into a coach bound for the major seminary at Marseilles to study theology. The atmosphere there differed greatly from the guarded life of the novitiate. He faced a heavy work load. English was essential for life in Canada. What a language ! All those exceptions !

He gained a reputation as a young man of strong faith who scrupulously observed the Oblate rule rather than as an exceptional student. He needed that faith to sustain him when family problems again engulfed his life. Frédéric and Mélanie were destitute from trying to rescue their father from disastrous business deals which often left them with barely enough to eat. Grandin could do little to help them except pray his father would stop throwing away what little money he had.

The days and weeks telescoped into a new seminary year. Grandin's health remained good despite a few bouts of illness. "I am sure just talking about the missions makes me well again." He began a steady advance along the stepping stones to the priesthood. He expected to be ordained a subdeacon in the spring of 1854, a deacon the next autumn and a priest in 1855. He was in for a surprise.

"Come in, Brother Vital. Sit here so we can talk." Bishop Charles Joseph Eugène de Mazenod, a man every Oblate respected and loved as the founder of their congregation, put Grandin at ease. Such private meetings with the superior general were rare for seminarians. Had someone in the Grandin family died ? Was there some reason to delay the ordination ? He remembered the crushing rejection by the seminary rector in Paris.

"What I am going to say may come as something of a shock to you." Grandin's hands tightened on the chair. He tried to force a smile but the tension was too intense to break his stare. He searched for some message in Bishop de Mazenod's face.

"Vital, your superiors believe you are ready for ordination. There is no reason to wait until the normal time. I have decided you will be ordained to the priesthood on April 23."

Grandin released his pent-up breath with a sudden rush. "I am so relieved. For a moment I thought there was some difficulty, that you might want to delay my ordination. I thought the date would be about this time next year."

"You don't understand, Brother. Your ordination will be this year. April 23, 1854. Prepare yourself to leave after your ordination for the missions in Oregon or Red River."

Grandin broke the good news to his family in a letter. "I am totally full of fear and totally overjoyed. Full of fear, because when I examine myself I feel wretched. Overjoyed, because I know God loves and cherishes the lowly and the humble; overjoyed, because I made my decision a long time ago to sacrifice myself wholeheartedly for him."

The six tall candles blazed on the main altar. Smoke from the smouldering incense in the thurible curled upwards, caught briefly in the sunshine that bathed the bishop's chapel for Grandin's ordination. Bishop de Mazenod entered in solemn procession. Grandin, dressed in a long white alb, carried the Mass vestments, symbol of his priesthood, which he would wear whenever the Christian community celebrated the mystery of the Lord's Last Supper.

"*Tu es sacerdos in aeternum.*" His confreres sang the psalmist's words Grandin had sought so eagerly to hear since his childhood when he delivered the mini-sermons to his family. "You are a priest forever."

After the laying on of hands by the bishop and other priests, Grandin's mind was a blur of images and words. "Congratulations, Father Grandin. May you have a long and happy life." The good wishes washed over him from all sides. Hands clutched his. Everyone wanted the new priest's blessing. After the joy of celebrating his first Mass the following day, he faced the wrenching prospect of a new round of farewells.

Life had been a series of departures for him, although this one was different. Was this the last time he would see his aging father and his sisters and brothers? Only God could know what dangers lay ahead in the North American missions where the only Europeans were explorers, fur traders and missionaries.

"I don't think I should go home before I set sail for America," he told Bishop de Mazenod. "That would save many tears for all of us."

"I don't like sacrifices that are forced on others. Go home and see your family and your friends," the bishop ordered.

Grandin returned to Le Mans, then journeyed from village to village where he had spent his childhood and teenage years. Abbé Sébaux, his former teachers and school friends welcomed the new priest. His family gathered at Sille-le-Guillaume to celebrate their joyful reunion with a son and brother who was now a priest of God. All of their anger and bitterness had disappeared.

"I am getting old," his father told him. "Soon you will hear of my death. Don't forget to pray for me. But leave home without fear. I prefer to see you and your brother Jean as priests rather than doing something else," the old man smiled, "even if you could pay me a pension of a thousand francs." His father had healed an old wound but the new warmth would make departure even more painful.

Vital and Jean breathed the salt air deeply as they stood on the dock at Le Havre. Smoke billowed from a funnel of the ship waiting to take Vital to a life of danger and hardship across the Atlantic. They talked quietly against a backdrop of longshoremen shouting to hurry the final loading of huge crates into the ship's hold. Other passengers delayed their final goodbyes as long as they could.

"Let's get out of this noise for a few minutes, Vital, while we still have time. I saw a church on the street leading to the dock. Surely we can find some peace there."

The two brothers knelt to pray for each other before an altar of the Blessed Virgin. Suddenly the ship's horn blasted a warning. Vital and Jean embraced for a moment, then hurried to the gangplank.

"I am sorry it must be this way. I know how much you want to come to the missions with me. Look after father and little Mélanie. Don't let him make any more bad deals." The two brothers laughed and embraced once more.

"Make sure you write to tell us about your adventures. The Lord be with you, Vital."

"And with you, Jean."

Vital turned to hurry on board. A warning blast from the horn signalled departure. He waved to Jean, almost lost in the crowd, as the ship maneuvered out of the harbor and into the English Channel. He held back the tears he knew would come once he got to the privacy of his cabin. From the deck, Vital watched the jagged coast of France slip behind the thick mist. The ship rolled in the short choppy waves. His heart ached for his family and the familiar life he must leave behind. But a whole new life of adventure waited for him on the other side of the Atlantic, a life demanding much personal sacrifice. He waited until the mist dissolved for a moment, revealing France's shore, a thin line between sky and sea. He waved one last time and walked below.

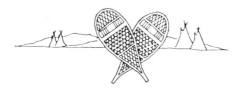

5

He Comes to Serve

THE SOUND of pounding hoofs startled Grandin. He twisted in the saddle to see the outline of a horseman riding hard to overtake him. The young priest's heart beat so rapidly he thought it would smash a hole in his chest. His horse, not needing any encouragement, took off with mane flying.

"God and your holy Mother, do something. I don't mind dying but if today isn't the day, do something quick."

He looked back in the dim moonlight. Was his attacker a Sioux? The members of the caravan had warned him the Sioux killed for the pleasure of it. Or was the horseman a member of the Saulteaux who excelled at night attacks, appearing from the darkness and disappearing again before their enemies could reach for a gun? He realized how foolhardy his decision had been to return to the last campsite to retrieve the forgotten keys to his trunk. Instead of waiting to make the trip in daylight, he had retraced the day's journey alone. Now in strange country he rode for his life. Only the rhythmic pounding of the hoofs broke the silence of the night. He took another look over his shoulder. Much to his relief he saw the horseman turn and ride away. Galloping his horse at full speed for a few more minutes, Grandin pulled up behind a clump of trees to rest the hard-breathing animal. The quick thump, thump of the young priest's heart slowly faded. He cautiously edged his horse back on the trail to return to his companions. He was learning an important survival lesson: as a stranger, you do not travel alone and you do not travel at night. "Thank God and his Mother. That was a close one."

The events of the past weeks flipped through his mind. He recalled his short stay in England, the Atlantic crossing to Montreal, the boat and train trips to Hamilton, then down through the United States to St. Paul, Minnesota, and the final leg of the journey to St. Boniface by ox cart. "Look out for the crooks when you hit Detroit," more experienced travellers warned. Grandin took no chances, standing guard over the baggage, hoping no one would suspect he was carrying a large amount of money. "I was loaded with money. I had money not only for my trip but money also for the mission. We had been told to carry it in special belts. But I made a kind of gold sausage with my handkerchiefs sewn together so tightly the coins didn't make a sound."

Now Grandin laughed at the thought of how his money had been so secure he couldn't get any of it free to buy food. While he and his companions were in the crowded American cities they survived for two days on two glasses of beer, afraid to show off any of their wealth.

Keys safely in his pocket, he arrived back at the camp in time for a few hours of sleep before the carts again creaked along the trail to St. Boniface, the Metis settlement the missionaries called "Little Paris."

When the seventeen carts rumbled down main street, their passengers dusty and weary from the long trip, Grandin spotted the beautiful cathedral — "just like home." No other building in the settlement came close to the church's grandeur.

The interior was painted and well kept. In contrast with the village, the cathedral was a marvel set among the primitive homes of the Metis. Many lived in lodges with gaps where the walls tried to meet but often failed.

St. Boniface was the seat of Western Canada's first Roman Catholic diocese, the base from which the Oblates roamed to serve the Indians, Metis and the few whites in the vast country of plains and forests. The missionary territory stretched a thousand miles west to the Rocky Mountains and north to the Arctic Ocean. Grandin's fellow missionaries had first stood on the grassy prairies in 1845. They soon fell under the spell of this land of extremes and abundance, although often they prayed for relief from temperatures that soared to 90 degrees Fahrenheit in summer and sank to 45 below in winter. Who could not stand entranced at the formations of ducks and geese stretching across the fall sky, quacking and honking their way south for the winter? Or be hypnotized as the sun flamed a brilliant orange morning and evening? Despite the beauty and bounty of nature that unfolded around them, the missionaries lived on the edge of hunger and poverty. Few people would believe that, to see stampeding buffalo, the great prairie providers of food, clothing and shelter. But Western Canadian nature dealt in excesses. Like those who had survived in the West for thousands of years, the priests and brothers enjoyed the feasts and endured the famines. Sugar, or "white stone," was allowed only when visitors shared the missionaries' table and on major feast days.

"We have only five missions in all this great territory. And you, Father Vital, are now one of our twelve apostles," Bishop Taché told him as they toured the St. Boniface mission. "This is the bishop's house. Over there, the parish rectory, a retreat house for prayer and meditation, a small hospital, a school and a community house for the Christian Brothers."

"You have done a lot in a short time."

"It is only the beginning. I have a vision of the Church flourishing in the West. The country is so rich, many will come."

Across the Red River at Fort Garry, Grandin could see the Hudson's Bay post. When the Indians came to trade furs for axes and guns, they made camp near the fort and at night gathered around their fires.

"If you want to teach them about Christianity, you must become one of them." The two Oblates watched a new group raise their teepee poles. "You know what it means, Vital? It means living with them and learning their languages."

"But how? There are no books around. I've scoured the mission. Who will teach us? We're all students here, except you, Excellency."

"I have the notes left by an old missionary. And I know someone who will help you, a Cree woman who is kind and patient."

Grandin started slowly, learning a few basic words each day, such as hand and arm. The woman was proud to have him for a student. She took her job so seriously that whenever he missed a lesson, no matter how good the excuse, it did not satisfy her. "You are lazy. I am going to beat you," she warned him.

Then he tackled another language challenge, to master the combination of French and Cree expressions used by the Metis. Hearing confessions turned into something of a guessing game. Many times he did not score too well. His language was far too polished for the prairie patois spoken by the Metis. "Judge for yourself," he wrote in a letter home. "If someone said in confession, 'I accuse myself of having somewhat badly juggled,' would you understand that he was saying he had bad thoughts?

"Before coming here I tried to speak French well. Now I try to speak it very badly."

Grandin spent the winter of 1854-55 like any country priest. "Today I baptized two little girls. One was forty-eight years old, the other forty-four." He worked steadily to minister to the Metis of St. Boniface and the Indian bands arriving to trade their furs.

The young Oblate paid the initiation fee of his first western winter. The price was two frozen ears when he failed to dress warmly for a funeral. Like all westerners, by March he wondered if winter would ever end. Finally, the warm southwesterly wind pushed back the Arctic front. The ice on the Red and Assiniboine rivers cracked and disappeared. The rampaging water rose menacingly, spilled over its banks in low spots, then flowed through nature's overflow channels.

"Well, Vital, I think it's about time for you to find out what life is like in the missions. Time to put Little Paris behind you. How about a trip on the barges to Nativity Mission on Lake Athabasca? It's a long trip, about 1,800 miles. I'll go with you as far as Île à la Crosse. Incidentally, do you know how it got that name? That's the place where whites first saw Indians play lacrosse."

Grandin would soon learn life in the missions was far from leisurely. In addition to all the natural hardships, isolation and poverty were the missionaries' constant companions. At best the mail came twice a year. His family and friends in France had written regularly during his year of language and theological study in St. Boniface. Now he would need that link even more. "Write to me often and as long letters as you can... Even though I am far from you, I love you all... The farther I go from you, the more I love you."

"Cast off. Put some muscle into those oars. We've got a long way to go before nightfall." The eight crewmen in each York boat dipped their oars into the water of Lake Winnipeg. So began his journey of forty days across lakes, down rivers and around rapids, the first of many such trips throughout the Northwest.

"That wind's blowing pretty good today. Once we get out from shore we'll put up the sail," the captain told his crew. "Then you can save some of that energy for the portages."

The two missionaries took their places, surrounded by bundles of tobacco, tea and guns to trade with the Indians at the northern forts. "A step down from the ship that brought you across the Atlantic. Well, get used to it. This is the quickest way to travel in summer. You'll see a lot of these barges."

"I'd love a place to stretch my long legs." Grandin squirmed to get comfortable.

"I'm afraid you'll have to wait until we stop for the night. Unfortunately they travel twenty hours a day to use all the daylight. Except for the portages we're on board until ten tonight. Did you bring your breviary, Vital?"

"Of course. Why do you ask, Bishop?"

"You'll see. But enough discouraging news for now."

Taché didn't tell his rookie traveller he had to fight boredom on these long trips. That's why he asked about the breviary, the book of psalms and prayers priests recite daily. Prayer would help pass the time. Despite the grandeur of creation all around them, the bishop knew even the hymns of praise and thanksgiving would grow a little thin until they eventually stepped on shore.

"Don't move, Bishop. There's a huge mosquito on your forehead."

Whack.

"Got him. I hope I didn't hurt you. He was huge."

The bishop rubbed his forehead to remove the squashed mosquito, then flicked it over the side. "Don't worry, I'll get my chance to return the favor."

With cassocks covering them from neck to ankles, the missionaries enjoyed some protection from the hungry insects. Vital Grandin had fought off mosquitos before, but none like the monsters diving at them from all sides. The priests used a concoction the Indians rubbed on exposed skin to repel the mosquitos and black flies. For added protection, Grandin wore a white polka-dot hat someone had given him. Not very clerical, but anything to beat the bugs.

"Don't go so close to shore. You'll rip a hole in the bottom. Then where will we be?" The captain shouted orders as the crewmen prepared for the first of thirty-six portages to bypass rapids and waterfalls. They maneuvered the barges near the rocks and overhanging trees, then jumped into the water to unload the cargo.

"Can we help?" the bishop asked.

"Hang on to your small bag, Excellency. We'll look after the rest," the crewman called out as he plunged into the icy water.

The portages were a break in the monotony for the two Oblates. For the crew, it was hard work hauling everything overland to where the water was calm enough to refloat the boats and continue the trip.

"Ready ? Let's load up." The men hoisted as many as six packs and strapped them to their backs. They picked their way along the rough trail, often for several miles, crawling through ankle-deep mud or clinging to steep slopes. Grandin marvelled at their strength and endurance, admiring their dedication to the dangerous work. Once the transfer was complete, the men leaned into their oars to find deeper water and a strong wind to propel them to the next portage.

"We will be in Île à la Crosse within hours. I am sure not a moment too soon. I have noticed, ah, a certain discomfort at times. Do you feel well, Vital ?"

"I did have a fever for a few days. Now I have a terrible itch. I've never felt anything like it before."

"I must ask you an extremely personal question. But first, my dear Father Grandin, there is something I must say. You are new to this country. You can't fully realize that certain precautions must be taken to protect your health. In the seminary you were taught to be properly and fully clothed in public, as a priest should be. The seminary is thousands of miles away. We are on the frontier, in a rough country with people who do not share the fine manners you were taught in Marseilles. Now the question. Have you changed your clothes, including your underwear, since we left St. Boniface six weeks ago ?"

Vital could feel his face grow warm. "There really is no place. Anyway, my clothes are all packed away."

"Say no more, Father, my diagnosis is correct. You have the traveller's companion — lice. Change everything when we land."

Grandin wanted to forget the experience but it was one more valuable lesson. The urinary ailment he developed on the trip was another affliction that would bother him often during his life.

"Look, Bishop. On the bank there, a welcoming party. A group of Indians. And there's Father Végreville."

The Indians fired their rifles into the air and yelled greetings to the men on the barges. The priest waved excitedly from the shore. The worst of the trip was over. The Red River brigade had arrived at Île à la Crosse on its way to Portage La Loche to meet the Mackenzie brigade travelling from the north. This was the connecting point where they swapped trading supplies for furs.

"Welcome, Your Excellency." Father Végreville kissed the bishop's ring. The two men embraced warmly. "A special welcome to you, Father Grandin. I see you kept your promise made that day at the novitiate. We are honored to have you both for a visit."

"I am on my way to Nativity Mission. But oh, how I need a few days on dry land. First, where can I change my clothes ? The traveller's companions are killing me."

"Breaking in another novice, I see." Father Végreville glanced at the bishop. The three laughed, then walked to the small church.

The Indians sang a hymn to welcome the bishop and the new priest. The long trip's strain and the sincerity of the celebration was too much for Grandin. He wept as the tension broke. Nothing in his seminary training or the long talks with the bishop had prepared him for this scene. Culture shock had hit.

Once he regained control, Grandin noticed the simplicity and poverty of the church. It was nothing more than a shed with parchment covering four windows. Someone had painted two of them red and green. The roof was covered with dirt and bark. The priest's house was the same rough construction.

"Often in France I had heard of the poverty of the missionaries as something to be admired. That was poetry... I would like people to see that poor church which is almost in ruins. When it rains, the dirt that stops the wind from blowing between the boards falls as mud."

Within a few days Grandin boarded the York boat again and the caravan headed northwest for three hundred miles to Lake Athabasca and the Nativity Mission. There could be few surprises, so he thought, after his initiation into mission life at Île à la Crosse. As mile after mile of dark green spruce and silver-white aspen slid by, his thoughts troubled him. He reconstructed the events of the few days at the mission. How could he, a product of the French culture of the nineteenth century, begin to understand the native approach? He had come to Canada to lead these people to his understanding of God and to demonstrate, by his life, God's love for them. Was that possible in the lonely and miserable conditions the missionaries must endure?

Again and again, he asked himself, "Am I happy?" Each time waves of nostalgia tormented him. How he wished to be home again. Memories of home and of his brother Oblates in Marseilles forced him to admit, "In any human way, I'm not happy. I don't come here with enthusiasm." Grandin was suffering a good case of homesickness. Each time he took consolation from one conviction he held above all others: that he was where God wanted him to be. These Indians were his flock. He would lead them to love and glorify God. "I have not come here to be happy but to make them happy."

The boats moved closer to the shore. He looked out over what seemed to be a great inland sea. "Lake Athabasca, Père Grandin. You have reached your mission," a crewman shouted to him.

There on the shore was the same scene as at Île à la Crosse — a band of Montagnais Indians to welcome the caravan. Three Oblates in their black cassocks stood with them. Their crosses tucked into their sashes, they had dressed in their best for this special occasion. Grandin waved. He was ready to go to work.

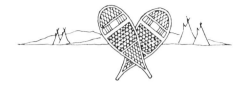

6

Your God Must Be Good

SMALL FIRES burned near the teepees to take the chill off the damp spring air. Grandin threw back the flap of a tent and stepped inside. Each evening he visited the families camped beside Nativity Mission on Lake Athabasca to comfort those who had fallen sick from the latest whiteman's disease. A woman knelt beside a boy wrapped in a blanket. She looked up for a moment at the young priest, not responding to his greeting. Then her eyes fell back on the child, agitated by the fever that burned his forehead. Often Grandin's halting effort to speak Montagnais, the second native language he was struggling to learn, produced smiles but not tonight. The number of sick was growing. Some children and old people had already died. The priest did his best to comfort the families but his resources were so limited he could do little more than remember the dead and the living in his daily Mass.

Grandin spotted another woman when he stepped outside the tent to continue his rounds. She was staggering toward the camp when she fell to the ground. He rushed to her side. "Here, drink this." She took a few sips from a bottle he offered. "Help me carry her to the mission," he called to a group of men. The woman had lost so much weight that one man easily carried her to the shed that served as the church. Her bare feet were cut and bleeding.

"My son, my poor son is dead. I had to leave his body on the trail. I have not eaten for six days. Three days ago I began to wander to find food. The trail still has patches of ice and snow."

"Are others sick in your camp?"

"Many are too weak to hunt. Some eat their clothes to stay alive."

"How much must people suffer, Lord? They are eating the very hides that cover their bodies." Grandin could feel his stomach churn as he prayed silently for the woman and her dead son. What could he do without medical supplies and food? He covered the woman with a blanket and begged God for help to end the epidemic.

He continued his rounds with frustration and anger gnawing at his stomach, the way it did each time he saw the unnecessary suffering of the Indians. He brushed away a cloud of mosquitos. The sun sat high in the northwest although the time was well past ten. In the light of the long northern evening, his eyes traced a line across the jagged pines and spruces. Through a break in the trees he could see the Union Jack fluttering over the Hudson's Bay post of Fort Chipewyan on Lake Athabasca, an important link in the company's well-established trading business.

In contrast with the tiny shack that was his church and house he saw the neat row of log buildings and the store house filled with the latest European goods to trade for furs. Smoke curled from the wood burning in the fireplaces of the staff houses and the residence of the bourgeois, the company manager, who indeed ruled the territory. Poverty, disease and starvation could not climb the log wall around the company compound. Instead, they were the constant companions of the Oblate missionaries. Grandin had to confront them alone. The other priests, Fathers Henri Faraud and Henri Grollier, and Brother Alexis Renard had left to work at missions farther north.

Grandin marvelled at the tranquil sight on that spring evening in 1856. In the fading twilight the fort stood as a symbol of the vast power of the Hudson's Bay Company. The company had pushed its trading operations far into the West and North with a string of forts, points of contact where the two vastly different cultures met. Fort Chipewyan had been an important base for the fur trade in the Athabasca area since the eighteenth century. The North West Company, a group of Montreal traders, used it as an operational center for their canoe brigades to collect up to 20,000 beaver pelts a year. Sir Alexander Mackenzie began many of his northern exploration trips from this fort. Then in 1821 the Hudson's Bay Company gained a monopoly in the fur trade with the absorption of the North West Company. With the last of the competition gone, the Hudson's Bay factor — "le bourgeois" as the French called him — was ruler throughout his territory.

The factors recognized the Indians and Metis as essential partners in the fur trade. Without them there would be no one to trap the animals, no one to transport the furs the thousands of miles by canoe and York boat to Montreal on way to the markets of Europe. The Indians had developed a trading economy among the main tribes thousands of years before the white man arrived. In particular, the Mandan tribe of the Plains Indians were skilled traders who could rival the whites in their shrewd dealings with other groups of Indians, understanding well the meaning of profit in any transaction.

The young Father Grandin quickly realized how much the missionaries needed the good will of the factors. The priests and brothers often used company boats for travel from one mission to another to minister to the scattered Indian tribes. The factors provided mail service, an essential link with families and friends in France. If the factors refused the hospitality of the fort, the missionaries could face exposure and even death. Although most of the officers of the company were Protestants, with few exceptions they treated the priests and brothers well.

The traders believed the missionaries were spoiling the Indians, but when there were disagreements and the threat of violence, the company men called on the missionaries to help settle the differences. Grandin was angered and dismayed over what he believed was the exploitation of the Indians by the traders. They treated some well but he believed the company men should do far more to assist Indians suffering the ravages of poverty and disease.

Walking slowly to his hut that evening, the only sound the priest could hear was the crack and hiss of green wood burning in an Indian's campfire. Two men sat near the doorway, their clothes dirty and torn. One puffed on a pipe. The smoke curled upward and disappeared. The man took the pipe from his mouth and passed it to his friend.

"Ma mère de Dieu." Grandin knelt before the crucifix and a statue of the Blessed Mother in the tiny chapel. "I beg forgiveness for my anger. Bless those in the fort. Blessed Mother, take the Indian families under your care. Give me the strength to match the traders' zeal. May I may work as hard for souls as they do for furs."

Grandin saw himself in a contest with the traders. He would have to match their dedication and their acceptance of hardship. "I learned more about obedience by watching them in their search for pelts than I did at the novitiate and the seminary," he wrote in his diary. "Haven't the souls of these poor Indians been bought by the blood of Jesus Christ?" Grandin knew he had no other choice than to accept the pain and hardship of missionary life, even the death of a martyr if that was to be God's will.

Summer's hot days and nights shuddered with the boom of thunder and the dazzle of lightening, then rushed into autumn. The missionary continued his struggle with Montagnais, learning the everyday words. He read from the scribbles on his pieces of paper, accepting the laughter of the old women. "Listen to this silly stuttering child." Comments like that did not bother him. To be close to the people he had to learn their language. He picked up other skills. He learned to mend fish nets. Fishing the waters of Lake Athabasca was as important to the Montagnais' food supply as baking bread for his relatives in France. He eagerly learned the Indians' techniques for surviving in the woods.

In turn, he became their spiritual teacher, explaining in simple terms the meaning of the Gospel message and how it could become part of their lives. He used to ring a small bell to call them to worship and give thanks to God. This practice got fouled up on occasion. Twice the Indians heard his bell ring at two in the morning. He explained sheepishly, "My watch fell asleep."

He made amends for the early wake-up calls by letting the community oversleep several times. He welcomed the few extra hours of rest. While sleep came easily after the strenuous work in the outdoors, he had trouble adjusting to the meager diet which depended on the success of the hunt. The Indians did make a meat-flavored paste from moss off the rocks. They called it "rock gut." Although no delicacy, it was tastier than boiling their clothes and eating them. The missionaries decided to add some variety to the daily menu by planting a garden. They grew wheat, barley and vegetables. Although an early frost caused some damage, they dug out a hundred barrels of potatoes, but only eighteen or twenty onions, three beets and one carrot.

"Père, come quickly. The boats are here," Brother Alexis Renard yelled. Grandin dropped his hammer and ran to the river. He counted ten barges, their oars breaking the water with rhythmic strokes, rounding a bend in the river and heading for the landing near the fort. The small group on the bank waved and cheered. The men returned the greeting, eager to dock and unload their cargo.

Mail from home — what a treat. Grandin rubbed his hands with anticipation. The one great pleasure left to him was to read and almost memorize the messages from his brother Jean, Mélanie and Abbé Sébaux. With only two deliveries a year, Grandin received enough letters to keep him up all night. "Keep writing long letters. If only you knew how happy I am to receive them," he would tell his family and friends. In return he maintained a flow of letters to them and to Church officials that would form a history of the Church in the West.

In his letters Grandin had described how difficult it was to teach the Indians, but at least an old man showed the young missionary he was making progress with the Montagnais. They were the most gentle and receptive of the northern tribes.

"The God you pray to must be very good since you are so good yourself," the old man told Grandin, surprising the priest with his compliment.

"Thank you, my friend."

"You talk to us, tell us many things about your God. You are a friend. The other whitemen want our furs, nothing else."

Grandin quickly gained the reputation of being a manitou — a holy man. "He knows everything. Nothing escapes him. He has it all in his book." Grandin startled one man when he asked him his name. "Why do you ask me? You know all things."

He liked the Montagnais, who were beginning to respond to his example of treating everyone with kindness and generosity. Once the Indians accepted his message of God's goodness and mercy, amazing changes took place in their lives. The simplicity of their approach was enough to stump the most experienced parish priest.

"Father, is it possible to punish my child on Sunday?"

"Now that I have made my First Communion, is it permitted to eat crow or dog?" Just try to refuse them such gourmet dishes!

One old man took the Friday abstinence rule so seriously he would go without food rather than eat meat. "I want to see God at all costs. I prefer to do more than not enough."

The most drastic change in the lives of his people was the way they treated the elderly, women and children. Other tribes killed older members who could not travel because they were too sick or crippled. The Montagnais simply left their parents behind. The worst treatment of all was saved for women. The men, so gracious with strangers, beat and even killed their wives when they tired of them. A Montagnais wife was not a person but an object to use. Wives and daughters made shoes and clothes for the hunters, skinned animals and carried supplies. Women had a slightly higher ranking than dogs. In fact, the word for daughter and dog was the same. Sometimes it was difficult to figure out which one the men were discussing. The women accepted their lives of misery and drudgery and the absence of all rights. For the men, acceptance of the missionaries' teaching demanded a complete change in attitude.

"Father Grandin, I understand now that women have a soul like us," a man told him.

"Why do you say that?"

"When you told us the Son of God had a mother taken from women, then I knew women must have a soul and a heaven like men. I want to be a Christian. You say a Christian must have only one wife. Tell me, how will I choose between my wives? Which must I send away?"

The man's wives pushed to the front of the small group. They stood beside their husband, one on each side of him. They stared at the young priest. Their faces showed no sign of the turmoil and fear that must have gripped them. The priest's decision would make one an outcast. Their future rested on the choice of the whiteman who stood before them.

"Black Robe, you say our husbands should treat us like they treat other men, not like the dogs that pull their sleds. Since you came with the command of your powerful God, they don't kill us any more."

The other woman broke in, "You have saved our lives. But now you want to take away the life of one of us. How will we live if our husband is allowed only one wife? Where will we go? Who will hunt for food?"

The three stood motionless, waiting for his answers. "I cannot tell you which wife to keep. You must decide."

The wind tugged at his cassock. He rarely wore it now, except when celebrating Mass or teaching those who came to learn about the new religion. He nervously fingered the cross in his sash. Smoke from a nearby fire made his eyes water.

"I have decided," the man said, pointing to the woman on his right. This one has a fourteen-year-old son. He will soon be a hunter. Then he can support his mother. Until that time, one of my family will look after her. This one must leave my teepee."

Turning to the other woman, he said, "She has small children. I will keep her." Grandin's shoulders slumped. He took a deep breath and thanked God that he had not been forced to make so difficult a decision.

Word of the missionary spread from one band to another. "Father, our hearts are dark. Give us the water to make our souls bright." Many of the Montagnais came to be baptized, although many lacked a full understanding of the meaning of Christian initiation. They understood one thing: no baptism, no entrance to heaven.

Grandin heard of a dying man who told his wife, "The ones who are baptized go with the Great Spirit. Quick, baptize me before I die."

"But what should I do? I have never seen anyone baptized."

"Take a bucket and get some water from the lake. Pour it on me."

The woman followed her husband's orders. "Again. Make sure I am baptized." She repeated the ceremony until he was soaking wet.

Grandin and the other missionaries marvelled at the simple faith of their new Christians. As the small flock grew, so did the demands on the missionaries to give the sacraments, to teach catechism and to be wise counsellors and peace-makers.

"After catechism people want to confess; my stomach wants to eat. After satisfying my stomach, I try to satisfy my penitents. I am at their disposal as long as they keep coming. All the time many of them wait in the hall. They get bored and impatient with the sins of others.

"Each one has an important message for me. An entire family has just arrived. I must touch the father's hand, the mother's, the boys', the girls', and even the papoose lying in a bag filled with moss on his mother's back. He is afraid of me and cries. I have to touch his hand or his mother won't be happy.

"After going through this ceremony, another one comes to me for powder and lead. An old lady wants me to fix her rosary; an old fellow wants a new one. A child wants a medal, one wants a cross, another wants a statue. A young man wants me to write him a hymn. His brother asks to be married. Everyone seems to be happy."

Grandin had shaken his homesickness. He wrote to his family, "My health equals my joy. Without bread, wine, cider, coffee or beer... working hard with my mind and often with my body, I am happy. Pray a lot for my Indians."

The Indians in turn showed their growing admiration and love for him.

"I wish I could meet your father," an old Indian told him.

"Why do you want to see him?"

"I would thank him for letting you come here to us."

"You will see my father in heaven."

"But I would like to see him in his lifetime so I could give your father my hat, one of the few things I have."

The gift of another kind of hat soon would shock Grandin and make him a Western Canadian for life.

Alexandre Antonin Taché, 1823-1894. Taché came as a missionary to Western Canada when he was still an Oblate seminarian. He became coadjutor to Bishop Provencher of St. Boniface in 1851 and two years later succeeded him. In 1871 St. Boniface became an archdiocese with St. Albert and the vicariate of the North as suffragan sees. (Original painting by Albert Ferland)

7

The Bent Reed

"**O**VER THERE. That's the camp of the Son of God," one of Grandin's two Indians guides shouted as he pointed to the teepees on a hill overlooking the English River near Île à la Crosse.

The priest urged them to hurry. "Come on, we've got to face Bear's Paw and stop him from misleading the Montagnais with his false claims that God has inspired him." Grandin rushed ahead up the hill, grabbing at small bushes to pull himself to the top.

"Wait. Wait," the guide called. "You must be careful, Father Vital. Remember what everyone has said. Bear's Paw wants to kill you. Please don't go into the camp. Even Father Végreville warned you your life is in danger. Be careful of this mad man."

Grandin did not reply. He continued to climb over the rocks and through the bush as quickly as he could. Bear's Paw was unpredictable but the priest had to take a chance to prove he was not afraid to die for his faith in Jesus Christ. Despite the need to concentrate all his energies on this threatening situation, he could not get his mind off the letter in his pocket from Bishop de Mazenod. Grandin now faced two crises in his life. He prayed God would deliver him from both but promised to accept God's will even if it meant death. As the priest and his guides entered the camp, Bear's Paw strode toward them to block their path.

"Stop. I command you to kneel before the Son of God."

"We will not kneel to you. You are not the Son of God. There is only one Jesus Christ. You are the son of Saskie, a Montagnais."

"I will prove to you I am God's only Son. I will show you Moses' tablets on which God wrote the Ten Commandments for his people. I will show you many other marvels. Then you will believe."

Men, women and children crowded around the two leaders and their supporters. Who would win this battle of words? They had believed Bear's Paw's story that he was Jesus Christ who had come a second time, having died once at the hands of the whites. Now the Montagnais were his chosen people. He had ordered them to destroy everything. "Burn your tents. Burn your canoes, your lodges and your furs. Then, only then will you be worthy to walk with the Son of God."

The Indians believed his arguments. They had listened intently to the missionaries' story of Jesus, how the whites had put him to death because they didn't believe he was sent by God. They didn't want to make the same mistake. Suddenly, Bear's Paw swung a neavy stick at Grandin, narrowly missing him.

"Don't be afraid," the young man's mother shouted at Grandin. "A blow with a stick is a mark of his love for you. He is forgiving you your sins."

Bear's Paw lunged at Grandin, grabbing his arms. The two struggled until the priest finally wrenched himself free.

He stood before the crouching Indian, one hand on his Oblate cross, the other raised, a signal to stop the attack.

"I am not afraid of your stick. I am not afraid to die. Least of all, I do not fear you for any reason. But you should be afraid. In a few days the whites will come to punish you for attacking me."

Bear's Paw rose slowly to his feet. He squinted, fighting to see against the blinding sun, his face glistening from the brief struggle. The people tightened the circle around the two men. No one spoke as the two leaders faced each other. Which one would the Great Spirit support?

"This, this Son of God," Grandin spat out the words, "if he is possessed by some spirit, then it is an evil spirit. He claims he can speak all languages. I have spoken to him in French and English. He can't speak either one. You are foolish to follow his advice. You have destroyed the few things you have. He claims he can grow grass and leaves whenever he wishes. Ask him to give you back so much as a handkerchief."

Grandin turned and left the camp with his guides. Later he got word that only a few of Bear's Paw's most ardent followers remained loyal to him. He had broken the young Indian's spell and influence on the people. A grateful Grandin was ready to forget the incident when he saw the people returning to the mission.

He had resolved one crisis but he still faced a second test. Returning to St. John the Baptist Mission at Île à la Crosse after his confrontation with Bear's Paw, he pondered the letter written by Bishop de Mazenod more than six months earlier. The Oblate founder had proudly announced to Grandin that Pope Pius IX had name him the coadjutor bishop of St. Boniface, as assistant to Bishop Alexandre Taché. "I can see you from here, stretched out on the ground, crying, as an expression of your humility, rejecting the episcopal crown that is going to be placed on your head. Put your mind at ease. It is placed on you by obedience. In the midst of the hardships of your ministry, it will seem more like our Lord's crown of thorns than the crown of the emperors of the world.

"You are a bishop by the will of the head of the Church and by my choice as your superior general. Be assured of God's grace and assistance. The episcopacy will become a way to salvation. The fruits of your ministry will become more abundant. Get rid of your depression and rejoice in the Lord."

Was he dreaming? Surely someone had made a mistake. He was only twenty-nine. A bishop! Grandin wrote to his superior, pleading with him to change the decision approved by Pope Pius. He offered his youth, his lack of experience, his incompetence, even his health, as reasons.

"I can't see anything that could justify such a choice, except the words of St. Paul, 'God chooses the weak of the world.' As for the qualities of a missionary, I have only the good will to serve God and to make people love him, which I share with my brothers. On top of that, I have long legs that make it easier for me to walk with snowshoes."

Bishop de Mazenod dismissed Grandin's objections. The Canadian bishops had made the choice, the Pope had approved it. "I do not accept your objections. I forbid you to offer any new ones. Come right away and do not wait until I am dead to obey my orders," de Mazenod ordered.

"*Te Deum laudamus...* We praise you, O God." The ancient hymn of praise rolled through the church of Saint Martin in Marseilles. Grandin bowed his head and prayed for his brother missionaries and for his people. On the day of his consecration, November 30, 1859, the rivers and lakes in the Northwest would be frozen, the temperature probably well below zero. He hoped his brother missionaries would pray for him at this critical moment in life. He stared at his new coat of arms hanging in the sanctuary, a public expression of his reliance on God and a promise to serve his people in Canada. The bent reed pointing toward the cross symbolized for Grandin the mysterious choice of those with seemingly few talents to do God's most important work. His whole life had been a bent reed. He read the Latin words, "*Infirma mundi elegit Deus*" — God chooses the weak of the world (1 Corinthians 1 : 27-28).

He knelt before the three bishops for the solemn consecration, the moment of receiving the fullness of the priesthood.

"Welcome, my brother," de Mazenod whispered. "This is one of the happiest days of my life."

The bells of St. Martin's rang out. Bishop Taché's assistant for the huge Canadian diocese walked down the aisle to bless all those who had come to share the joyful event. Before the new bishop's many friends could offer their good wishes, Grandin hurried to embrace his brother Jean and Abbé Sébaux.

"Thank you, my brother, and you, Abbé, for guiding me so carefully to this day. Never stop praying for me." As they talked, Grandin heard a voice call from behind.

"Must I now call you 'Your Excellency'?" Grandin whirled around. Mélanie gave him that look he knew so well from the days when big brother and little sister played in the fields. He threw open his arms and hugged her warmly. "Well?" she insisted.

"You know bishops can give dispensations. You have my first."

The two laughed and joined a small group of priests from Le Mans and the diocese of Laval where Jean was a parish priest. They wanted to congratulate the new bishop before he returned to the missions of North America. Little did those present know how much he would ask them to sacrifice for his people and that they would be partners in his mission endeavors for more than forty years.

After the celebration of his first Mass as a bishop and a round of receptions and banquets, de Mazenod took Grandin on a tour of Catholic organizations in Marseilles. "I want you to meet an apostle," he told the many groups. He treated Grandin like a favorite son, making sure he had everything he needed. When they sat down to eat, de Mazenod put several pieces of bread near Grandin's plate. The older bishop had noticed how much Grandin enjoyed bread, a staple in France but a delicacy in the missions. "Poor children. When I think of their hardships, the fork drops from my hand," de Mazenod wrote.

The founder of the Oblates expressed his admiration for Grandin in a letter to Bishop Taché. "Oh, this excellent Bishop Grandin. What a perfect missionary! He is esteemed and revered wherever he goes. All of his thoughts are for the greater glory of God, the salvation of souls and the interests of his far-off missions."

While some men may have welcomed the adulation, Grandin had difficulty accepting the honors heaped upon him as a bishop. Once he had completed his tour of Marseilles, he was anxious to leave for Le Mans to spend what time remained with his family and friends. The round of receptions and celebrations made him afraid to come home as a bishop lest somehow it would so set him apart he could no longer be a member of the family.

"Vital, you must take your miter with you. The bishop's hat is a symbol of the state to which God has called you. I would rather you go home without your shirt than without your miter," de Mazenod gently but firmly ordered him.

"The victim will be ready for the sacrifice," Grandin said as he packed not only his miter but also his crozier, the staff bishops carry on ceremonial occasions.

"Make sure you use them," was de Mazenod's parting comment.

If Grandin thought he would escape a similar outpouring of attention at home, he completely misjudged his family and friends. His aging father was speechless. He cried when the two embraced. It was the same at the Précigné seminary. The teachers and students treated Grandin as a hero. Here was one of their own who had survived the dangers of the great unknown mission land. Even more amazing, here was a bishop who was only thirty. They eagerly gathered in the large study hall, enthralled by his stories of hardship and the many funny things that happened just trying to cope with daily living. But Grandin told them all that was nothing compared with the joy of seeing the people slowly respond to the missionaries' teaching about God and the Church.

"Bishop Grandin, we have a gift to remind you of your student days at Précigné." The rector handed him a box. "Our students hope you will use it at least once a year. Perhaps even more often." Laughter turned to applause when Grandin lifted the lid and held up the bell he had rung many times as a student to call the seminarians to class and to the chapel.

There was even more applause when the bishop thanked the students. "I remember well the custom that allows visitors to grant holidays. You can count on my gift in return."

He received other gifts, one far more startling than the bell. During a visit to the seminary of Mayenne he had told his stories about life in the diocese of St. Boniface. Following the custom on such occasions, the rector responded but in a most unusual way.

"Your Excellency, I wish to present the students in our philosophy class. Take your pick for work in the missions."

Grandin was stunned momentarily by the directness of the offer. The young men said nothing to the young bishop facing them. He remembered the day another young bishop had visited his seminary, and how direct contact with Taché had been the start of his own missionary career. "I will take these two," he replied, placing his hands on the shoulders of the two students nearest to him. They were the future missionaries, Fathers Hippolyte Leduc and Prosper Légéard.

In the midst of what had become a triumphant tour, an old enemy was waiting. He had all but forgotten the frail health that dogged his student days and almost cost him his priestly vocation. Now as a bishop he felt a compulsion to accept every invitation to speak in churches and schools, wherever people wanted to hear about the missions. But he couldn't keep up the demanding pace. Illness forced him into bed for more than a month, and he regained his strength just in time to board a ship for Canada.

His departure was far different than the first time he had left for the Red River. After five years experience in the Northwest, Grandin now left France with confidence and determination. Proudly, he travelled with two new priests to share the mission work, Father Émile Grouard, his cousin and a future bishop in northern Alberta, and Father Jean Séguin.

Despite Grandin's eagerness to return to his missions, he found the farewells as painful as ever. "This is the most difficult moment in the life of a missionary," he wrote his family. Once the coast of France had faded for the second time in his life, he turned to the demands of his new position.

"Enjoy the sea breeze while you can," he advised his companions. "Summer in the West is like the oven your mother used to bake bread. And wait until you see the mosquitos."

The mosquito attack on the defenceless travellers bound for St. Boniface from St. Paul, Minnesota, was so ferocious at times it was impossible to stop for meals.

Boom. Boom. The cannon roared out a greeting to the travellers. "Look there, a buggy." The priests and brothers and the five Grey Nuns from Montreal shaded their eyes to see two horses trotting toward them. "It's Bishop Taché," Grandin cried out to the others. "He's coming to escort us to St. Boniface."

The buggy pulled up near the lead cart. The two bishops stepped down quickly to greet each other. "Vital, my new bishop. Welcome home. We have been expecting you for several weeks. I see you have brought some helpers. Are they strong enough to take our tough life?"

"The trip to Île à la Crosse will be the test. How well I remember."

"Tell me about yourself. You look tired. Are you well?"

"I fell ill at my home. It was the excitement, the demands to go here and there. But you know what it is like for a bishop, especially one home from North America. Just give me a few days."

The two bishops climbed into the buggy to catch up with all the news. The rest of the group followed in the other buggies, their baggage piled around them. The parade moved off to cover the short distance to St. Boniface where the residents were waiting to welcome them. "We don't fire the cannons and ring the church bells for just anyone," Taché said. Grandin's ashen color startled the older bishop but for the moment he decided to say nothing. The carriages rolled into Little Paris on the Red River to the cheers and shouts of the crowd.

Grandin rested from the arduous journey for three weeks. Rather than regain his strength, he became much weaker. For the last ten days before his departure for the gruelling nine-hundred-mile trip to Île à la Crosse he could not get out of bed. As the time grew short he struggled to his feet to offer Mass. "If only I can stand at the altar, I'm sure I will feel much better." But even with the help of two priests, he almost collapsed before completing the service.

"You stay home and I will make the trip," Bishop Taché told him several times, finally pleading with Grandin not to leave St. Boniface.

"You know I must go. If you keep me away from the missions it will kill me."

When the time came to leave, Bishop Taché took him as far as he could by buggy. "I beg you, Vital. For the last time, let me go in your place."

Grandin refused the offer. The two men shook hands and Taché watched as his friend slowly boarded the York boat. The oarsmen cast off and headed north. The new bishop prayed, "Lord, I'm ready for whatever you send."

8

Into the Storm

GRANDIN carefully folded his purple cassock and placed it in the bottom of a bag. Only on rare occasions in the next three years would he need to wear any clerical finery. A small group of Indians, Oblates and Grey Nuns prayed during a final High Mass for God and the saints to protect their new bishop on his travels. The date was June 2, 1861. Grandin was ready to say "au revoir" to Île à la Crosse and head north to visit the Catholic missions. No matter how great the personal cost might be, he was determined to go to Nativity Mission on Lake Athabasca, Our Lady of Sorrows near Lake Athabasca, St. Joseph Mission at Fort Resolution on Great Slave Lake, Sacred Heart Mission at Fort Simpson, St. Raphael Mission on the Liard River, St. Thérèse Mission at Fort Norman and Our Lady of Good Hope Mission at Fort Good Hope.

"I beg you, pray that God will bless my trip," he told the group. "I will give you a final blessing, then I must be on my way."

"Good luck, Bishop. God be with you," they cried as he clasped their hands once more, then settled into the canoe. He crossed his long legs, trying to make himself comfortable in the cramped space. He took out a pen, a bottle of ink and several sheets of onionskin paper from a wooden box. He was anxious to begin the detailed record of one of the most daring expeditions of a life constantly pitted against landscape and sky that seemed determined to block his every step.

For a man raised in the more moderate European climate, Grandin had quickly learned to cope with the Canadian discomforts of cold and heat and the torment of black flies and mosquitos. While others might turn away from such a trip in fright, he felt compelled by his obedience to God's will and his trust in providence to press on. Submerged rocks waiting to tear the bottom from his canoe and sudden violent storms on northern lakes could not lessen his desire to visit the remote missions.

"I have tried to use every moment to the point that I believe I can say during nearly thirty-eight years spent in the Northwest, I have not lost with my knowledge one single hour." The statement in his diary was a rare comment about his own dedication to mission work.

On this major expedition down the Mackenzie River he took three Indian guides to lead the way through the largely uninhabited country. One of these was Jean-Baptiste Pépin, the bishop's trusted travelling companion although only twelve or thirteen. Together they would face death at least twice on their travels. Grandin looked on Baptiste as a prodigy. He had little formal education but learned some French and English and spoke several Indian languages. When they arrived at a settlement, the youth quickly rounded up the local Christians, stood in as a sponsor at baptisms and kept stray dogs out of the tiny mission churches. Grandin wrote glowingly about Baptiste's worth to him. "He will be my servant, my nurse if I am sick, my valet, my cook and my sacristan (one who prepares what is needed for Mass and other religious ceremonies), my little vicar."

The joyful reunions with his fellow missionaries renewed Grandin's spirit and strengthened his health. But his diary reveals he was also troubled by the poverty, the isolation and the enormous task of establishing the Church in such a remote area. June 15, Nativity Mission: "Here I am back in my old mission, where I had my first missionary experience. I can't hide it from you, my dear family. I write to you to forget my sorrow."

To add to his burden, a devastating blow threatened the future of the northern missions. Word came that a fire had destroyed most of St. Boniface, the storehouse and lifeline of the northern missionaries. "Fire has destroyed everything: the bishop's house, the cathedral, all the furniture, all the provisions for the northern missions, everything, absolutely everything has been destroyed. The losses are enormous, irreparable in many ways.

"In spite of our poverty we had accumulated a lot of wealth. It was from there we received all of our things. We can say this fire has reached us in Île à la Crosse and in Good Hope. There isn't an inch of material left to clothe thirty-three missionaries — bishops, priests or brothers."

But he could not complain about their great misfortune when so many reminders of the Indians' extreme poverty faced him every day. One morning a little girl who was sick came to the mission for some medicine. One of the priests gave her what he had but warned her about a rule of the Church. "Be careful not to take any medicine or eat anything before you go to Communion."

"Father, don't worry. I won't eat. There is no food in our tent, no food at all."

The Oblates were one with their people. Gladly sharing a diet which rarely offered food as basic as bread, they survived the brutal north wind in porous shelters. Slowly they persuaded Indian men to discard tribal warfare and cruelty to women. The missionaries' one aim was to lead the Indians to an acceptance of the Christian faith and its values. Grandin was impressed by the progress the Oblates and Grey Nuns were making. "Indians have a very strong faith. In spite of their ignorance and simplicity, their conduct could make many people in France blush with shame, people who are more educated than they, who believe themselves to be pious and good Christians."

Even with the faith blossoming, Grandin and his missionaries could not relax. As he worked his way north from mission to mission, the bishop feared the gains made with such sacrifice could be lost to the rapid advance of Anglican and Protestant clergy. The Christian denominations, their unity shattered by old disputes, battled for the Indians' loyalty. Like rival fur traders, the priests and ministers raced to remote areas to claim new converts. Europe's conflicts had spilled over to the British colonies. Grandin's dedication to the papacy and his desire to establish the Roman Catholic Church throughout the Northwest made it impossible for him to view the competing clergymen as anything other than false prophets.

The denominational race began in earnest in 1858 when the Anglicans made their first attempt to establish a mission about two hundred miles north of St. Boniface. Until then, the North had been the territory of the Oblates who had established missions as far north as the Arctic Circle at Fort Good Hope. The odds were loaded in favor of the Anglican and Protestant clergy. They had the support of the powerful Hudson's Bay Company, established by the British Crown. When the Anglicans failed to expel the Oblates from the North with a petition, they convinced the Hudson's Bay factors, whose word was law, to refuse the Catholic missionaries shelter at the forts and transportation on company boats. Bishop Taché convinced the governor of the Hudson's Bay Company to reverse the orders issued by local officials. Despite the change in company policy, Grandin and his missionaries felt uneasy when they had to depend upon the Hudson's Bay men for assistance. They grew to distrust the company's officials.

"What can be expected from such a man who tells you that he loves you as an individual but detests you as a public person?" Grandin responded. "The arrival of the preachers forced us to attempt the impossible."

By that time the northern missions needed a bishop of their own. The territory was too large for a roving bishop like Grandin to serve adequately. Also, the pressure from the other denominations was forcing him to start preparations for someone who would take charge. He found a site west of Great Slave Lake on the Mackenzie River to establish a new mission, a hundred and sixty miles northwest of St. Joseph's Mission at Fort Resolution. The missionaries depended so heavily on God's providence, then Providence it would be called. Here a new northern bishop could make his headquarters, but the thought that he might be appointed that bishop worried Grandin. Left to himself, he believed, he could never establish a diocese along the Mackenzie River.

As Grandin walked along the bank of the Mackenzie, he could visualize the crops growing in the black soil. He knew the river would produce plenty of fish. He inhaled the perfume of pine and spruce trees, ideal for construction and firewood. "Yes, we will build a new mission here."

In the distance he could see a Hudson's Bay boat heading for shore and recognized Roderick Ross riding in the stern. Stepping ashore, the clerk called out, "Bishop Grandin, are you stranded here? If you want to come with me, you must hurry. We can't stop for long. By the way, I have some mail for you."

"Mr. Ross, I have something to tell you. I am happy to find myself here with you." The company official smiled. It was not often the Catholic priests spoke so warmly to him. After all, he was one of those preparing the way for the Anglican missionaries. The Hudson's Bay Company wanted the Anglicans to have for their headquarters the site Grandin had chosen for the Providence mission.

"Mr. Ross, you represent the first magistrate for this whole country. I was told you consider this spot to be ideal for a mission. I wish to advise you that I am taking it over."

"But Bishop Grandin, you don't know what you're doing. How are you going to live here?"

"I have nothing to lose. We will try for a year or two. We will study the terrain to see what we can build."

"You and your missionaries are wasting your time. You can't compete with us. You aren't rich enough."

"Mr. Ross, in this country wealth, as you must have learned, is not enough to survive. You must be ready to sacrifice, to sacrifice everything, including your life. That is what our missionaries are doing."

"Bishop, we are ready to leave. Are you coming?"

"Thank you for the kind offer. I think I will stay here for a while to take a good look at my new property." As the boat moved slowly away from the bank, Grandin's party pitched a tent and erected a large cross to mark the site of Providence Mission. Then he sat down to read the latest news from France, news that disturbed him. Bishop de Mazenod was ill and Pope Pius was under political attack from Italian patriots.

Grandin continued his expedition northward with a visit to Fort Simpson, hub of the fur trade with its mixture of tough adventurers, then mission by mission to Fort Good Hope, his final destination before the winter storms along the Mackenzie Valley made long-distance travel dangerous. By early October, sharp chunks of ice battered their flimsy canoe. One smashed the bow, leaving them stranded without patching material. Fortunately a Hudson's Bay boat appeared with a load of fish bound for Good Hope.

"Hel-lo, hel-lo. Over here," Grandin and his men yelled. "Our canoe is smashed. Can you pick us up?" Despite the hostility toward the missionaries, company men would not leave them stranded. Once the boat had maneuvered to the bank, the missionaries abandoned camp and climbed aboard.

Down river they spotted a tiny shack on a cliff overlooking the river — that was Good Hope Mission. Falling snowflakes softened the breakness of the scene. As Grandin climbed the hill to the mission, Father Jean Séguin ran to meet him. The two broke into tears. "It is the usual arrival ceremony," the bishop recorded in his diary.

"But where is Father Grollier?"

"Don't be surprised if Father Henri is late. And if he doesn't speak for a while, when he manages to get here."

Before he could ask for an explanation, Grandin noticed an old man leaning heavily on a cane, slowly climbing the hill. "Is that Father Grollier?" Grandin could hardly say the name. "But how? What has happened? He is so young. But now so old. Is this what the mission life does to us?"

"I know what you're thinking. A young man, just like you, still in his thirties. Life here offers so little, God demands so much sacrifice. Father Grollier's health is broken, gone."

Grandin ran to help the priest who motioned he would climb up the embankment by himself. Meanwhile, Brother Patrick Kearney appeared from inside the tiny building. He had been plastering the walls with mud. "Bishop, welcome to our mission." He dropped to his knees. "Please, I would like to have your blessing." Once on his feet again, Kearney embraced Grandin and tears glistened on their cheeks. "You must stay for the winter. Soon it will be too cold to travel."

"Of course I shall stay. But first I must see where you live."

"Do not expect too much," Séguin warned as they ducked their heads to go inside. Even the primitive conditions Grandin had seen in his trip throughout the North could not match the one-room hut that measured only eighteen by twenty-two feet. The three Oblates used it for a church, living quarters and workshop.

One thing bothered Grandin, the absence of a tabernacle in which to keep the Eucharist, a place where the missionaries could pray and gather strength. He helped them cut trees to build a small chapel. There they set up an altar with a plain box as a tabernacle and decorated the surrounding wall with a fish net and some religious pictures. "The ceilings were so low that they could stand erect only between two joists. When we were in bed we enjoyed watching the northern lights through the cracks in the roof. But these holes also let in the snow and the icy winds," he told his diary.

Father Grollier walked slowly into the room and slumped onto an old crate. The three insisted Grandin sit in their one chair. Once Grollier had rested for a few moments, he was able to announce some good news. "We are going to have a real feast. We have a beaver and two partridges, thanks to Father Séguin's hunting eye."

"Please don't think me ungrateful. But you enjoy the delicacies. I would prefer some of your fish. Believe it or not, I have eaten nothing but meat for more than two months."

"And I will make some crepes," Kearney added.

With that, Séguin reached for the small supply of candles they burned only at Mass. "We've never used one at meals in all the time we've been here. Tonight is different. This is an occasion."

The candle finally sputtered out in a pool of wax. The four Oblates lingered at the workbench that doubled as a table. No one wanted to end this rare evening that warmed them long after the fire was only a glow. For the moment their most persistent enemies, isolation and loneliness, had fled into the night. In the dim light the four swapped stories, some tragic, others humorous, about life in the missions. They listened to every scrap of information Grandin could give them, plans for a new bishop to take charge in their area, news from their homes in Europe. The one disturbing note in the night of friendship was Grollier's wracking cough. Grandin glanced often at the skeleton which had replaced the man he had known as young and robust. Two huge eyes returned his glances. The bishop knew he had to act. Father Grollier was dying.

"I worry about your health. Believe me, I know what it means to be sick. You must do something for your own sake and for the sake of our struggling Christians. Unless your condition changes for the better, you must be ready to travel on the barges when they leave for Île à la Crosse. There the Grey Nuns will look after you. The food is much better. You will regain your stregth."

"Please, Your Excellency. Allow me to stay here in this mission. I can teach catechism to the Indians, then Father Séguin can travel to the isolated tribes. Don't worry, providence looks after everything. Missionaries usually don't have long illnesses."

Grandin did not force the priest to leave Good Hope. Father Grollier died about two and a half years later. He was thirty-eight. The Indians and Metis came by canoe and on foot to pray for the priest who loved them so dearly that he chose to stay at the expense of his own health, a decision that meant his death.

Grandin grieved for his friend and confrere but he was convinced no sacrifice was too great for himself and his missionaries to make in order to make the faith grow and flourish.

His Happiest Days

THE INDIAN GUIDE hit the ice a glancing blow with his axe. A large chunk of it broke off and he threw it aside, opening a narrow pass for a few feet through the ice dunes. The weight of Grandin's pack with his few clothes and his breviary grew heavier as he watched the dogs strain in their harness. A second guide finally twisted the sled through the narrow opening.

Grandin's party was retracing its way south along the Mackenzie Valley after spending three months in Fort Good Hope during the bitterly cold winter of 1861-62. He never confronted harsher conditions than they now faced. The older Indians searched their long memories for a winter worse than this one. Grandin could have waited out the bitter weather at Good Hope, instead he felt he must move on. The temperature on the Mackenzie River regularly dropped to 50 below in the dusk and dark of the almost unbroken Arctic night.

The ice dunes stood as one of nature's spectacular creations. When the river began to freeze in the autumn, the current flowed over the surface, then froze and piled up in the icy contortions high over the heads of the travellers. Passage was possible only if they were willing to chop a route through the dunes and help their yelping dogs drag the sleds.

At times Grandin and his companions crawled on their hands and knees, then slid down icy inclines to find their way through the maze. "Try the way to the left," he called to the lead guide.

The man stared at Grandin, then grabbed the bishop's nose, twisting it and then gently rubbing a handful of snow over his face. Grandin realized the man was not suddenly insane or playing a childhood game. "You're getting frostbite. Be careful or your nose will fall off."

Grandin knew the danger of allowing exposed flesh to freeze hundreds of miles from the most basic medical treatment. Soon after, gangrene would set in, then death for the traveller. He and his missionaries wore no distinctive clerical clothing when they were on the trail in winter. Survival dictated their outfits.

"Apart from a flannel shirt I wear only leather: long moose trousers, a second caribou shirt with the fur inside, plus a moose overcoat." He kept his hands warm in what he called his "two bags of white bearskin" hanging around his neck on a string. Because of the danger of freezing a finger, he hung his bishop's ring on the same cord that carried his Oblate cross. On his head he wore a beaver-skin hat covered with a shawl to protect his face and neck. His eyes peeked out from a hood fringed with fur and wreathed with ice.

If the cold didn't lull travellers into tempting but deadly sleep, ravens were ready to pick them apart. During a break in the trip to Fort Norman, Grandin watched a flock of ravens skim low over him. They brushed his clothing with their wings until he frightened them away by shouting and slapping his mitts. He had heard the native guides tell chilling stories of the birds eating starving dogs and horses.

After a day of struggling through the ice dunes with only chunks of frozen meat to sustain them, the men dug a pit in the snow with their snowshoes. Spreading their blankets on spruce bows, they would crawl in, hoping to trap enough body heat to allow them to sink exhausted into sleep for a few hours before another day on the trail. "When we had eaten, talked enough and my men had finished their pipes, we knelt down to say our prayers... I always kept my socks on as well as my moccasins and my coat during the night. When we woke up in the morning, we often found ourselves covered with snow."

Grandin would lie under the blankets in the snow pit, too tired to fall asleep. The memories of the past three months at Good Hope collided in his mind. He prayed for his missionaries and the dying Father Grollier. "God bless their work. They sacrifice so much." On clear nights he lay in the cold watching the northern lights dance their spectacular patterns, whirling and darting across the sky. He would trace their designs until they lulled him into a fitful sleep that ended far too soon. Many of the Indians and Metis faced starvation that brutal winter of 1862. He heard one story of a hunger-crazed father who killed and ate his five-year-old daughter. More common was the family, without food for days, eagerly devouring two pairs of leather shoes left by a fort employee in one of the camps.

Grandin's daring journey that winter amazed even the most experienced northern travellers. He accepted its hardships as the price he must pay to be a bishop in a mission territory. By the time he got to Fort Simpson, a distance of almost seven hundred miles, the worst was over. "Thanks be to God, the most difficult part of my trip is done. In spite of so many difficulties, my health and my strength are intact. More than once, completely tired out and almost discouraged, I told myself I am through, that I just can't do any more. Always, I was able to convince myself that a person is capable of doing much more."

"Bishop Grandin, here is something guaranteed to put a little spring into your step. The winter mail has arrived.

Look at all the letters for you." The factor at Fort Simpson held up a large package.

The bishop hobbled to the counter, his feet aching with blisters from ten days on the trail. Snow blindness from the early spring sun's reflection on the white landscape left him squinting, his eyes burning so badly he could hardly read his mail. One letter shocked and saddened him. Bishop de Mazenod, the man who had guided him through all of the stages of his religious life, was dead. "With him I lose the most loved father, the most devoted benefactor of our missions."

As a final sign of friendship and union with his congregation's founder and his friend, he knelt and opened the gold case he had carried from Fort Good Hope. After removing the consecrated bread and receiving Communion, he prayed fervently that the bishop might find peace and happiness with God. Later, Grandin said he felt he should be praying to de Mazenod, rather than for him. Grandin had little time to grieve. He was far too busy coping with the complexities of missionary life.

"Did I have to give him a name?" The chief of the Dogrib Indians at Fort Rae on one of the northern arms of Great Slave Lake had come to announce the death of his baby son. In the absence of a resident priest, the chief had baptized the baby himself. The missionary did not want to upset the man but his experience had taught him to be ready for the unexpected from new Christians who took such a direct approach to their faith.

"Giving him a name is a good idea. But even if you didn't, everything is fine as long as he was baptized."

"I gave him a name. The best I could find."

"What name did you choose?"

"Jesus Christ. What better name to call your son?"

"You named your baby Jesus Christ? Of course, that's a fine name. But after this, don't use that name for your children. That is God's name. Not man's name."

The chief listened attentively. "I did it to help Jesus Christ remember the boy better."

The Indians' approach to Christianity was direct and uncomplicated. Sometimes Grandin wondered how well his new Christians understood the meaning of the sacraments. Another incident showed there was no doubt they realized baptism was essential to enjoy life after death. Two women came to him to announce their babies had died. Unlike the incident with the chief, these children had not been baptized. That was no problem for them. "Can you baptize their bonnets?" the mothers asked.

He was pleased with the steady growth in the number of people who accepted the faith. So many of the Dogribs came for Mass in the small hut which was both residence and chapel that they had to crowd around the altar. They were devout but their lack of reverence at times annoyed Grandin.

Once during Mass, he turned around to the congregation to say "*Dominus vobiscum...* The Lord be with you."

"I saw right near me a big simpleton calmly smoking. He had lit his pipe from the candle on the altar. I stretched my arms farther than I normally would and slapped the pipe from his mouth. He was greatly embarrassed and so was I. After Mass I excused him, assuming he was a newcomer. I scolded the others for not telling him how to act."

For Grandin to call anyone a simpleton was out of character. Usually he showed great patience in dealing with the Indians who were so new to the practices of the Christian religion. Surely the bishop had a right to be cranky once in a while. When the weather allowed him, he moved from mission to mission, much of it on foot, across some of the most treacherous terrain in North America. But far more serious trials would test him when Providence Mission (today Fort Providence) became his base. Father Émile Petitot and Brother Prosper Boisramé had made a start on the new mission.

"Congratulations, Father, you and Brother have done wonders. What a sight to see a new log church and a house. It will soon be September. We can expect snow anytime once the leaves fall."

"Take a closer look, Bishop. It needs a lot more work if we are to survive 40 below this winter." Brother Boisramé wiped the sweat from his forehead. "We have to fill the holes between the logs. The ground is our floor. What I wouldn't give for doors and windows."

Grandin went to work with the brother and priests, mixing a batch of northern plaster — grass and mud. The application was a hit but mostly miss affair. "I'll throw some more and pray it sticks."

"Bishop, you've got as much mud on your clothes as we have on the walls. The wind may blow through the cracks this winter but it certainly won't touch you." Joking helped ease the tedious labor but these patient men also were practical. They knew how much a few simple tools could speed and improve their construction jobs.

Grandin's anger flared when the boats arrived without any supplies. "Neither tools nor merchandise nor food," he wrote in his diary. "No doubt because of a lost letter, the bishop has received nothing, absolutely nothing." He considered abandoning the project for a year, until he could get what they needed to build the future headquarters for Bishop Henri Faraud who would become the first bishop of the Northwest Territories in 1862.

"I thought we would be tempting God's providence to continue," he told the missionaries. "Instead, I've found a way around our difficulties so the work will continue."

"A way around? What do you mean? Can you somehow pull the supplies out of the sky?"

"Not quite. We have taken a vow of poverty. In practice this means we share with each other. No one owns anything. Each one owns everything."

"Yes, yes, I'm beginning to understand." Father Petitot, the missionary at St. Joseph's in Fort Resolution, nodded with a smile that grew broader as Grandin outlined his plan.

"While the barges are here, we have the supplies for Good Hope, for Slave Lake, for all the missions. We will take a little from each. They must learn to share so we can survive."

A year later, Grandin came as close to exploding as he did at any time during forty years of frustrating work on the frontier. The barges arrived with little for the construction work at Providence. As in all ages, the Church of the 1860s had its foul-ups. He poured out his frustration in a letter to Bishop Taché.

"What do they expect me to build with? I wasn't sent an axe, not a single file, not a single one of all the tools I asked for. What did I get to enrich my chapel? Three cords for my alb (the long white vestment clergy wear at Mass is tied at the waist with a cord). Nothing I can wear on my back. I'll have to travel in my purple cassock.

"One box contained pieces of dishes, rotten hosts and many damaged things. One metal plate is worth six broken ones. Not a single pocketknife. We have come to the point of having to beg our young man for buttons, whenever we lose one off our pants..."

Cooling down enough to warn Taché to handle his letter only with the tips of his fingers, Grandin added, "I would like people to understand what we are exposed to when they forget things."

Despite the irritation of their supply problems, the missionaries finished the construction job. Grandin even converted a barrel into an easy chair in the sparsely furnished residence. Enough work, it was time to celebrate. What an excuse to replace the daily diet of dried fish with fresh meat. But he decided to pass when he learned the main course was a faithful old dog, Cabri, served with white sauce. Obviously, sauce was the secret to make such delicacies palatable. On those special occasions the diners needed a distraction, something to cover the harsh realities of life. They used this culinary diversion often. "On a certain feast day, the menu consisted of an ancient crow the dogs had refused to eat, served with an exquisite sauce."

He enjoyed the crow and admitted he would eat dog meat if he were starving. Starvation was a constant fear during that first winter at Providence. After hectic work to repair the mission's fish nets plus the problems of trying to fish below the ice, the catches suddenly increased and game became plentiful. The sudden food surplus gave the missionaries the opportunity to show the fur traders they needed each other for survival. The men at the fort had often warned Grandin he would die of hunger because the Church lacked the wealth to support its missionaries adequately. Now it was the missionaries' turn to rescue the traders. Grandin spotted two Hudson's Bay barges trapped on the Mackenzie River by ice packs. They were trying to move farther up river to load supplies of fish and game. Failure meant the people at Fort Simpson would face starvation. He eagerly gave the company men 1,500 fish and five hundred pounds of meat. "To help others is always a pleasure. But for me, there was an additional pleasure." For once, Grandin was not forced to beg for food and shelter from company officials.

During such meetings, some company officials liked to talk religion. They chided Grandin for believing what they considered absurd mysteries, such as the Trinity — three Persons in one God. While he provided theological arguments, young Baptiste gave more convincing explanations.

"Look all around us. What is that ?"

"It's snow, of course," the factor replied as the three walked along the river on a clear winter day, right after a blizzard.

"And underneath ?"

"Ice. We all know that, my friend. What has that got to do with your belief in that nonsense you call the Trinity ?"

He couldn't throw Baptiste off his point. "And underneath the ice ?"

"Water. But..."

"There it is. All three — snow, ice and water are different but all the same. All water. That's about as close as we can get to the Trinity. Understand ? You must admit it does make sense."

The company men acknowledged a different force powered Grandin in his daring trips up and down the Mackenzie Valley. They heard of his narrow escapes when in the winter of 1863-64 he was lost twice in a month on the ice of Great Slave Lake. As his three-year expedition to visit the northern missions neared its end, much of the earlier religious hostility disappeared.

One company official wrote of the bishop's courage in a land where rugged men were admired. "I know that your unequalled patience and your unfailing courage have aroused the admiration of all the officers in the district, without even mentioning the esteem and affection that your personal qualities have inspired in all of those who live along the Mackenzie River." Yet while there was growing admiration among the whites for Grandin and the Oblates, some of the Indians looked down on people who were poorer than themselves.

"The Indians are gone," Brother Boisramé announced. "They left early this morning for their camp on the lake. What can we do?"

"Gone. But why would they leave?"

"They say we are so poor we don't have any tobacco to give them."

"But everything is for them. We bring them God's word."

Grandin felt as though someone had punched him in the stomach. All the work, all the suffering meant nothing to them. "Of course we will follow them. Get the canoe ready. Quick, Brother!" They paddled hard against the current. A brisk wind tried to turn the canoe sideways into the high waves. "Look there, Brother. I see them on the shore." The Indians disappeared into the trees to hide in their lodges. The canoe stopped with a lurch on a sand bar.

Grandin tramped through the bush to look for the Indians, leaving the brother to beach the canoe. He spotted the Indian camp, a dozen teepees around a large fire pit. A dog barked, then another to sound the warning as the bishop approached. No one came to greet him. He stood near the pit, wondering what to do. He knew the Indians must be hiding in their teepees but he wanted them to come to him.

"I know. A Montagnais hymn will get them out." He sang as loudly as he could. Slowly the Indians appeared and crowded around him. "I should not be the one who comes to you. You should come to me. You say why should we go to him. He doesn't have any tobacco to give us. It is not to give you tobacco that I have come from so far."

Some grumbled, "If he doesn't have tobacco, what has he got?"

"Other strangers have come to take your furs and give you tobacco and clothes in return. I have come to teach you the way to heaven. I kissed my old father goodbye nine years ago. It was hard for him to see me go. But he agreed so I could come to you. Now I will write to my father to tell him the Indians don't want to listen. That they look down on his son. He will die of grief. You complain I don't give you any tobacco. You will smoke with the evil spirits. I want to save you from that."

An old man pushed his way through the crowd. "Let me speak. Let me speak." He walked slowly to the spot where Grandin was standing. Slightly stooped, a blanket covering his shoulders to keep out the spring chill, he was one of the elders of the tribe. Stopping in front of Grandin, he stared at the bishop through eyes with crows-feet that disappeared under long grey hair.

"Father, don't judge our hearts by our words. We do not know you well. The other white people come to us like a mosquito. It comes, sucks your blood, then leaves. The whites take what they want. They return when they want more. They give us something in return. But you, you are so poor, you give us nothing, not even tobacco to smoke. Now we understand that your gifts are more precious. They will last long after the smoke from our pipes has drifted away."

The old man turned to face the crowd. "Hurry, take down your teepees." His words, firm and determined, broke across the heads of the men and women. Even the children stood frozen by his voice. For a moment, the gentle rustle of blowing leaves was the only sound. "Put everything into your canoes. We are going back."

The crisis over, Grandin returned to Providence to continue the work of extending the Church throughout the North. He travelled from one mission to another, encouraging his priests and brothers. Sixty years later in 1922, Bishop Émile Grouard of Athabasca wrote in his diary about the year of 1864 which he shared as a young missionary with Grandin at Providence Mission. "We were never so happy in all our lives. You should have seen us climbing up our ladder made of rope ends, then crawling on all fours into our places, perhaps one over the other.

"Sometimes a foot or a leg went very far down through the floor. Planks were apt to move a bit. They were not nailed down for the very good reason that we had no nails... Not one of us would have changed places with the shah of Persia."

By August of the same year, Grandin was back in Île à la Crosse for the first time in more than three years. Almost immediately his health broke down. He was spitting blood. The Oblates and Grey Nuns were alarmed by his condition. They had seen him ill before but never as weak as he was now. Three years of exhausting travel and poor food had left him drained and listless. Even his hair was showing some grey. He spent most of the next winter in bed.

10

Test from God

"**F**IRE! FIRE! Please, Bishop Grandin, come quickly. The house is on fire." A young boy ran into the room in the Grey Nuns' convent at Île à la Crosse where Grandin and the other missionaries were finishing their dinner. "Flames are shooting out the windows."

The laughter ended abruptly. "The children, our books, all our supplies are in the house." Grandin rushed outside. "Quick, let's save what we can." The priests and sisters ran after him. Brother Bowes was already trying to douse the flames with a hose and a small hand pump.

"I think I can put it out but we're short of water. If only we had more water," the brother yelled when he saw the others.

Grandin yanked open the front door of the residence. Dark acrid smoke billowed out. Flames attacked his clothes, forcing him back. "We must save the Blessed Sacrament. Go around to the side." Once inside, he saw smoke curling from under a door. He ran down the short hallway to the chapel, put his arms around the tabernacle (the box that housed the consecrated bread), heaved once, then again. With a grunt he lifted it from the altar. The smoke was much thicker now. Flames hissed as they ate through the green wood. The new two-storey building had been their pride and marvel — a residence, a school, a house for some of the Grey Nuns. Their precious tools and leftover materials were in the flames. The destruction of the building would be a serious blow to the missionaries' plans to expand their work among the people around Île à la Crosse, setting back their work at least until the next year when they could start rebuilding.

"Over here. The door is here." Grandin stumbled through the opening, barely able to hang on to his heavy load. The smoke seared his throat, making him cough and gasp. Tears ran down his cheeks, then turned to ice water in the March air. He slumped over and a brother grabbed the tabernacle, carrying it to the church.

"The powder. We must get the powder out before it explodes," someone shouted.

The missionaries kept a supply of gunpowder and shot for hunting. They used most of it to trade with the Indians in exchange for leather clothes, provisions, and services such as guiding.

"The window in the storeroom is blocked. We can't get in. There's too much smoke. We don't have time to move it out," a priest warned. They ran around the building, looking for another way in.

Grandin ordered, "Stand back as far as you can before it blows and kills us all." When he turned to run, he noticed one of the brothers lowering children from a second-storey window. The blankets around them were burning.

"Bishop, Bishop," the brother yelled from the window between gulps of fresh air. "The children, I'll throw them to you." Grandin saw his figure outlined against the flames. The brother carefully dropped the screaming children to the waiting arms of the missionaries who rolled the children in the snow to smother the flames. When the last one was safe, the brother disappeared for a final desperate search. Then he climbed through the opening and hung for an instant before dropping with a splash into the slush below. Moments later the floor caved in. Once it was gone, the walls leaned, shuddered, then collapsed in a shower of sparks.

"Look out! The powder's going to blow any second."

The ragged group fled in terror, afraid the explosion would win the race for the safety of the frozen lake. They wrapped the children with what was left of the blankets to protect them from the biting wind. The little group stood shivering to watch the flames steal their hopes, the building gone which they had thought would serve several generations of young people.

Then a new danger caused even more terror. "The fence, there between the house and the church. It's on fire. If it goes, the church will burn. Put out those flames before they get to the church," Grandin ordered. They followed the bishop's command, ready to tear down the fence with their bare hands to save the church.

The powder exploded, scattering debris and sparks over the huddled survivors. Suddenly the wind shifted. Instead of driving the flames toward the church, they moved harmlessly toward the lake.

By nine o'clock the residence and school were a burned-out shell. The timbers, cut and raised with so much labor and love, glowed like the dying embers of a huge bonfire to mark a happier occasion. Pools of water from the snow melted by the intense heat soaked everyone from the knees down as they searched for anything of value not devoured by the flames.

"Let's not stand around here or we'll all catch our death of cold," Grandin told the group of stunned adults and crying children. "We must go into the church to warm up and dry out. Above all else, we must give thanks to God. We will dedicate our new building to Saint Joseph."

"Dedicate our new building to Saint Joseph? Can you be serious, Excellency? Sister Marie-Anne Pépin told Grandin what most of the others were thinking. "Saint Joseph let our house burn down. If we give him any encouragement, who knows what will burn next?"

Grandin smiled at the sister. Of course she was upset. But the bishop had suffered too many times to become angry with what he considered to be God's will, no matter what the personal cost. "The saints know how to accept crosses. Always there are two sides. Those things which make me suffer most often turn out for the best. Let's see what good God can produce from this evil." In a clear, strong voice he led the survivors in a hymn to give praise and thanksgiving to God.

Sister Pépin shook her head. "Who can win against a man like this? He turns every defeat into a victory." She sang as loudly as the rest.

Grandin was up early the next morning, poking in the debris to salvage nails and anything else of use. Two stone chimneys and several charred beams were all that remained. Despite his resignation to the cruel events of the night before, the fire devastated him. So much of the material gains in the past twenty years had been lost in a few hours: furniture, a library, tools, his own diary which he had written so faithfully in canoes and in snowbanks. "I don't have a handkerchief to wipe my tears." Replacing the destroyed items would be costly for the poor missionaries, but at least transporting them would be much easier the second time. Grandin's new trail now connected Ile à la Crosse with Lac Vert and Fort Carlton, a distance of about two hundred miles. The rest of the way to St. Boniface was still mainly by water. For years, canoes and barges had moved most of their goods. Grandin's dream of a road carved out of the endless bush and around lakes and prairie sloughs was the start of a new era. Now caravans could haul equipment, such as stoves, to make the harsh life more bearable. Officials of the Hudson's Bay Company at first had frowned on the road plan. Improved transportation would help free traders compete with them. The Bay had a monopoly in the Northwest, one it intended to keep. Somehow the bishop not only convinced company officials that the project was worthwhile, but they even paid part of the cost. When it was finished, Grandin went on a buying spree in St. Boniface. "I even bought some cats."

The fire drained him of his vitality and some of his determination to fight against all odds. Publicly and privately he accepted the tragedy as God's will, but he had to find the resources to regain the momentum his missionaries had built up through their hard work. Perhaps Bishop Taché could open some doors, introduce Grandin to people who would be willing to replace at least some of the twisted tools and blackened books and, most of all, to donate money to begin rebuilding.

Grandin watched St. Boniface come into view. Workmen were rebuilding the cathedral and other buildings destroyed more than four years ago by another devastating fire. "Somehow we must start building with stone. Wooden buildings invite fires. Bishop Taché will understand how heavy my heart is. He has gone through all my suffering and more."

"What's that, Bishop?" one of the boatmen asked.

"Nothing. I was just thinking out loud."

Once the men tied up the barge, Grandin carried his bag down the narrow gangplank and hurried along the river bank to the mission. Taché was bent over a hoe in the garden, planting potatoes. "Make sure you get them the right side up."

Taché looked up and began to laugh. "I don't believe it. But yes, Vital, it is you." The two men shook hands firmly and embraced warmly. "What brings you to St. Boniface? I thought you would be heading north on another of your lengthy adventures. But how fortunate you have come. There is a letter here from the superior general. If it's what I think it is, you will soon be on your way with me to the Oblate general chapter in France. Now tell me, what brings you to our big town?"

"My Bishop, I have bad news. Our new residence in Île à la Crosse burned to the ground in early March. We lost everything except the clothes on our backs. Our books, everything is gone. I have come for advice, to ask your help to lift this great weight from my soul."

"Come inside, Vital. You must be tired. We will have tea and something to eat. Tell me, was anyone hurt in the fire?

How did it start? I will tell you what we did after our mission burned down. And then I have something to discuss with you — a new diocese in the West. The Church is on the edge of great expansion. We must be ready for whatever comes."

The door closed quietly behind the two as Grandin began his story.

"I think we are agreed, Vital, that there is little we can do to replace what you lost in the fire. Europe is your best chance. You see, God has arranged things so you can tell your story there."

"I agree. I will take my problems to our congregation. So many have so much in Europe. Surely they can spare something for our poor missions." He drained the last drops from his tea cup and picked at the remaining bread crumbs on his plate.

"That's real flour, not fish roe like you use in the North. Here, have another piece." Grandin could not refuse. "Now the plan. The whole West to the Rocky Mountains is too large for one diocese centered in St. Boniface. Just as the northern missions were split off, there must be another division farther west. You built the seat of the diocese at Providence Mission for our confrere, Bishop Henri Faraud. It's time to think about establishing another diocese. You, my friend, are the prime candidate to be the bishop of the new vicariate of Saskatchewan."

Grandin had feared the day would come when European immigration to the West would force him to head his own diocese. "I have long prayed that I would die before you so I would not have to become the bishop of St. Boniface. I want only to be your assistant, to spend my time with the Indians. Surely, surely someone else is better able to lead than I am."

"Think about it, Vital. Bishop of a new diocese may not be so bad. It would be a lot better than succeeding me if I should die. St. Boniface is in the middle of a political tug-a-war with all the talk of annexation by the United States. Settlers are moving into our area. The new diocese is the frontier. You like the life. Think it over."

"I won't be able to think of much else."

"Take advice from someone who has had more experience in Church politics. We are participants in the birth of the Church in the West. Oh yes, we have a voice in what happens. But the final decisions, as you know, are made at higher levels. The Quebec bishops are planning French and English dioceses and one farther West for Indian languages. It's all in their hands. There is no need to worry. What happens will happen. You and I can't do much to change the course of history in 1867."

"Of course, you're right. But the thought of heading a diocese worries me greatly."

"Vital, where is your trust in God's providence? Forget it for now. Let's talk about our trip to Europe. We sail May 25. Paris is our first main stop for a meeting with the superior general. Then Rome, for the eighteenth centenary of the martyrdom of Saint Peter and Saint Paul. Autumn for the general chapter. Then time to tell your story at home to raise the money you need."

When Grandin arrived in France, the doors closed gently but securely. His experience in Paris was typical of the reception he met. "I am sorry, Bishop Grandin, but you know how bad conditions are in France these days. Unemployment is high. There is poverty everywhere. Many people have very little to eat."

"But I ask for so little. Just the opportunity to preach in some of the churches of this diocese. An appeal for my poor Indian missions. We have suffered a disastrous fire. We lost everything. You are the bishop's secretary, a word from you."

"My dear Bishop Grandin, there is absolutely nothing I can do. The bishop sends his regrets. There are so many people coming into the diocese to promote good causes. We can only do so much. And besides, the order from the Propagation of the Faith in Rome does not permit special collections. Au revoir, Your Excellency."

"Thank you for your patience. There are other bishops. Perhaps some generous souls will help." Grandin tried not to show the rejection he felt but his shoulders drooped as he walked away.

Several months passed, months filled with small dinners given by people eager to listen but not ready to give. "My friends, I have come to speak to you tonight about a land of which you hear very little." Promises to arrange interviews with high-ranking government officials, who were always in meetings, produced little. "I gather barely enough to keep myself in poverty. But next to nothing for my missions." However, his sincerity and persistence did catch people's attention. He became the nineteenth-century version of a media star. If talk shows had existed in his day, he would have been in constant demand. Louis Veuillot, the leading journalist in Paris, was one of the bishop's biggest fans. He told his readers Grandin's story of complete self-sacrifice in the cruel and demanding conditions of mission life in North America. The bishop's adventures were read by thousands in *L'Univers*, Veuillot's newspaper. "There is no poetry in these missions. There is only prose — cold, dull, horrible prose."

Veuillot's reaction: "As we listened to him, this thought came to our minds — the Catholic Church has the secret of making heroes..." Grandin's listeners responded to the stories of travel by frail canoes, shooting through swollen streams to take the sacraments to the bedsides of dying Indians. "I have collected 70,000 francs in cash," he reported to Father Joseph Fabre, the superior general who succeeded de Mazenod. "People have given me things for my missions worth another 30,000. But above all, thirteen men, priests, brothers, laymen. They all want to work in my new diocese." Twice the size of France — could anyone imagine a diocese that large? But for some unknown reason Church officials in Rome held back the necessary documents to establish it officially.

"What could be holding them up?" he asked Father Fabre.

"First, I think you had better go to Rome. See if you can get an audience with the Pope. He will understand your impatience and start the wheels rolling. Remember, they're always thinking about eternity. If it doesn't get done today, well, in God's good time. Light one of those prairie grass fires under them."

"Do you really think I can do anything there? I'm not anxious to go, the expense and all." But he took the superior general's advice, packed his bag and caught a train for Rome. He stopped to stare at St. Peter's magnificent dome as he hurried to the papal palace. Rome and Île à la Crosse, centuries apart, yet they shared the same Gospel message. Would the Pope understand?

"Bishop Vital Grandin, the Holy Father will see you now." The Pope's secretary was a young Italian monsignor about Grandin's age, but his cassock with purple-trimmed buttons and a purple sash contrasted sharply with the missionary's worn clothing. "You will have about fifteen minutes. I have the papers for your new diocese. This way."

As the tall, narrow door opened, Pope Pius IX came from behind an ornate desk. "Bishop Grandin, I hear many things about you and your work in Canada. Welcome to Rome." For a moment Grandin was so in awe of the Pope he had difficulty speaking. "Come, Bishop, sit here. First, business. Then we will discuss life in your missions. I know that is your favorite topic."

"Your Holiness, the bishops of Quebec have petitioned for a new diocese in the West but nothing seems to be happening. I am anxious to return home with some indication of the future."

"Of course, we all want some hint of our future. Rome's ruins were the hopes of men like you and me. Life is uncertain, even for a Pope. I was forced to flee this city once. As for your own concern, don't worry, I will take up the matter of the new diocese. I understand the cardinals are reluctant to approve it because only three bishops signed the petition. A mere detail. You will submit your resignation as Bishop Taché's coadjutor. You will become the new bishop of Saskatchewan. I will see the papers are ready before you leave Rome."

"Thank you, Holy Father. There is another matter. I wish a special permission for my missionaries. That they may keep the Eucharist without burning a sanctuary lamp." Grandin watched the Pope's smile turn to a scowl. Pius, a nobleman, believed his clergy should keep the Church's rules.

"No, my Bishop, I shall grant that request only in times of persecution. You haven't reached that stage yet."

Grandin didn't know what to do. Dare he argue with the Pope? He believed rules were made to serve people, not to hamper the work done with so much sacrifice. He must speak up. "Holy Father, it is true we are not persecuted. But we have so much to suffer, the cold, poor food, and we do without many things you would take for granted. If you take God away, what will become of us?"

"Not even one candle? A piece of candle?"

Grandin's forehead furrowed. "Yes, if we must. But it is just one more expense. We must conserve everything to survive."

Attacks from Italian politicians had taught Pius the importance of survival. "You have my permission."

The Vatican grapevine buzzed steadily after Grandin's meeting with the Pope. Cardinal Alessandro Barnabo, who was handling the paper work for the new diocese, told Grandin, "I don't know what you said but you missionaries know how to get what you want."

"I don't have any secret approach. He is a most kind father."

"He wants you to accept these gifts. And beautiful gifts they are. First, a chalice for your celebrations in the missions. That's not all. Your most kind father has sent you a ciborium to keep the Eucharist in, without a burning candle I might add." The two men stared at each other for a moment, then broke into loud laughter. They shook hands warmly. "May God keep you safe, Bishop."

Grandin began a round of wrenching farewells in 1868 before boarding a ship once again for Canada, and he embraced his aging father for the last time. When he docked in Quebec City in May of that year, he learned the Canadian council of bishops was meeting to settle the details of the new diocese in the West. St. Albert won over Edmonton as the headquarters of the diocese. Just seven years before, Bishop Taché and Father Albert Lacombe had chosen St. Albert as the site for a new mission overlooking the Sturgeon River.

Oblate priests and brothers were already at work, but Grandin knew there would be few resources to start the new venture. The caravan trip from St. Boniface to Île à la Crosse underlined his most immediate concern — how to support a new diocese with no financial resources of its own. Every mile which the carts jolted and creaked along the trail he realized was costing him more than the combined railway and ship fares from France. To save money, he left many personal belongings behind, including ten boxes of tobacco, ten barrels of sugar and nine other bales of goods. They would come later when he could pay the shipping charges.

A month after the caravan rolled out of St. Boniface, the travellers were still on the trail. Grandin searched the sky for signs of better weather. Night after night rapidly moving storms had battered the travellers. Thunder ripped and roared as the sky opened to let the next lightening bolt zigzag to the tallest tree. No one slept until the storms themselves seemed to grow tired an hour before dawn. And then, they slept fitfully as steady drizzle soaked clothing and blankets, adding to their irritation.

After morning prayers, Grandin warned his missionary recruits of the danger ahead. "We must move cautiously today. You can see the mud is so deep our carts are sinking to their axles. One is broken. We don't want to break any more. The grass is slippery on the hills. Even worse, we must still cross the North Saskatchewan River. The banks are steep. Pray God will guide us to solid ground."

Crack. The drivers snapped their whips as the carts started another day of slow and torturous travel. Everything went well at the river crossing. A boat ferried the carts across the swirling brown waters to a flat spot where the oxen took over for the climb up the bank.

"Hey, look out," one of the drivers yelled. "I can't hang on to this one. He's heading for the river." The animal had turned suddenly and stampeded with the cart and its nine hundred pounds of cargo. The cart plunged into the water and sank before anyone could stop it.

"Quick, save the trunk. It has the gifts from the Pope." That wasn't all that went overboard. Grandin lost all his clothes, family pictures, tools and other items so badly needed for his missions. They camped on the river bank for several days to search downstream for the lost items. But as quickly as they had fallen into the river they had disappeared, gone forever. Accepting the latest blow with the same resignation as the disastrous fire the year before, Grandin wrote in his diary, "It was God's holy will. In spite of prolonged efforts, nothing was recovered."

Eventually the group split up, sending some of the priests and brothers west to St. Albert, while Grandin and the others bumped and jolted their way north to Île à la Crosse. A month later he too would make the westward trip to begin a new phase of his life as first bishop of St. Albert.

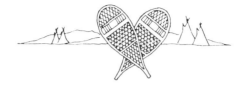

11

Death Roams
the Prairie

THE METIS HORSEMEN fired volley after volley into the air as they sliced through the thick morning fog into full view. Grandin's cart stopped with a jolt, throwing him forward. In the distance a cannon rumbled, either a threat or a salute. "Have we stumbled into an Indian fight?" the bishop yelled, grabbing the driver's arm.

Before the driver could answer, at least thirty men, all shouting, surrounded the bishop, their rifles still belching fire. One of them led a riderless horse. The bishop held up his hand in greeting. He searched their faces, looking for someone familiar, such as Father Lacombe. His uneasiness drained away as the group's leader explained their purpose.

"Your Excellency, we offer you this horse to ride to the mission. It is just three miles away," the leader of the group

117

announced. The excited horses snorted, heads bobbing. Their tails swished as they stood waiting, never quite still.

Grandin breathed deeply to calm his excitement. "Good. At last we are getting close to St. Albert." It was October 25, 1868, the day of a new beginning for Grandin, the day of his official reception as bishop of St. Albert. He mounted a horse decorated with red, green and white pompoms and rode to the bottom of the mission hill where more Indians and Metis shouted a welcome. On the way up the hill, the group paused at the first of several arches, built for the occasion, to listen to speeches by Father Albert Lacombe and local Metis leaders.

Lacombe stepped from the group to greet the bishop. "Welcome, Bishop Grandin. We have looked forward to this day for a long time. Our mission may be poor but it is rich in spirit, eager to spread the Gospel to the Cree and Blackfeet."

Grandin's eyes scanned the small crowd, rugged hunters and trappers, a woman with a young boy lifted high to see what all the excitement was about. Here were his people, men and women ready to follow their new bishop. "Thank you, my friends. The good God has much for us to do." After a short rest he would be ready for work.

The overcast sky gave way to brilliant sunshine on his first official tour of the mission perched on a hill. Shoes crunching the dry yellow leaves, he walked near the edge of the valley, his eyes tracing the course of the Sturgeon River which meandered from Big Lake in the west, and disappeared to the east for a meeting with the North Saskatchewan. "And look, a bridge. A real bridge, thanks to Father Lacombe. No more tipped carts, at least here."

He counted forty homes in the valley below. Fields with rich black soil, fenced and dormant after the harvest, showed that missionaries and residents were struggling to build a community among the spruce and poplar.

"Well, Bishop, what do you think of our valley?"

"Father Albert, what beautiful land you have here. You chose this site well. And here it is almost November with no snow. We northerners aren't used to such luxuries."

"You will feel right at home in a few weeks when the first blizzard roars out of the northwest and the temperature dives below zero. But the big difference is in the people. Many here do not accept the teaching of the Gospel."

"I haven't had much to do with the Plains Cree and the Blackfeet. You're the expert. How do they get along with each other? How should we approach them?"

"The Crees and the Blackfeet are enemies to the death. Somehow we must find a way to end the attacks and, worse, the massacres. The Blackfeet are much harder to convert than the Crees. The only way is to travel with them and, more important, live with them."

"You mean live with them all the time?" the bishop asked.

"We call it 'going to the prairie.' They spend four mounths every spring and summer chasing the great buffalo herds. Hundreds of hunters take their families, even their children, to help with the slaughter of the great beasts. I must become one of them."

"God's blessings go with you, Father. Is there any point in telling you not to take too many chances? We need all our priests."

Grandin spent Christmas and the cold months in St. Albert. Conditions reminded him of the winter in Fort Good Hope. Only this time, instead of four people, eight were crammed into a long shed that served as home, church and workshop. They slept on the floor, wrapped in buffalo robes. Bread, which he liked so much, made an appearance only on feast days. The Oblates survived on pemmican, the Indian meat concoction which was pulverized, boiled in grease and allowed to dry in a sack for a year. One of the missionaries wrote to his family, "It is then chopped with an axe and has all the delicious flavor of a candle. Besides this, we have meat which has been dried in the sun and is almost as tender as leather." Despite it all, the priests and brothers stayed healthy and even gained weight. They nicknamed Grandin "Canon" when he put on a few pounds, a reference to well-fed parish priests back in France.

The missionaries spent the winter months of 1868-69 planning how to use their meager resources for the people. They decided St. Albert needed a new church to serve the five hundred Metis who lived around the mission. The missionaries looked also to the future when they would need more room to serve the thousands of immigrants who would settle the prairies, once the Northwest Territories was annexed by Canada in 1870.

The missionaries recognized time was not standing still for the Indians and Metis. Events were hurrying the time when the native people would have to adopt some of the settlers' lifestyle just to survive. For centuries the prairie gave the Indians everything they needed, such as the buffalo which provided much of their food, clothing and hides for their teepees. Soon that resource would disappear. Bishop Taché estimated hunters had slaughtered a million animals a year for the last quarter century. The Grey Nuns were already teaching native children new skills: farming, woodworking, some French and English — which the missionaries believed the next generation would need when the buffalo roamed no more and a change in Paris styles would threaten the fur trade.

Grandin worried too about the survival of his vast diocese which stretched from the American border to the Arctic Ocean. One of the most serious threats came from an unlikely source, his old friend Taché. Through Taché's decision, the most beautiful and prosperous mission, Our Lady of Victories at Lac La Biche, was lost to Bishop Faraud's northern diocese.

Bishop Taché had established the mission as a supply center for the Far North. When the Oblate superior general approved the boundaries of Grandin's new diocese, Lac La Biche was in the territory. Under strong pressure from Taché, Grandin reluctantly agreed to give up the mission, at least temporarily. "I would never have thought this was to be done with so much hurry," he wrote Taché. Grandin desperately needed the resources of Lac La Biche to relieve some of the extreme poverty his Oblates and students suffered at St. Albert.

He did not have so much as a cent. Worse still, his work was hampered by the weight of a 10,000 franc debt he believed was owing to the Propagation of the Faith, the Vatican office responsible for the missions. He had borrowed the money for emergencies. His desperation leaps out from the pages of his diary. "The state of my finances frightens me, almost discourages me. What can I do to save more? I haven't any idea at all."

He begged for help from the Metis families. "I have six students to take care of. I am asking you for skins so that pants can be made from them. You find it more important to build a lodge with those skins. One can always go without a lodge, not without pants." He must have been happy to see 1869 come to an end. Surely the 1870s could not rival the '60s for disasters? The list included a fire that had destroyed all the feed for the cattle at one mission. In St. Albert, another blaze destroyed the winter supply of firewood, plus 40,000 shingles and most of the lumber for the new church. Early frost had blackened the crops, leaving nothing to harvest. Accidents had cost the mission seven horses and two oxen.

He reacted as he always did in the face of personal disaster. In a letter to Father Joseph Fabre, he wrote, "The wealth of the world alone would never be enough to complete the work of God. In our missions we must learn to do without." He was no armchair leader, brooding over his bad fortune. He laced on his snowshoes or rode on horseback for hundreds of miles to minister to the Indians, the Metis and the few whites. His ministry extended far beyond gathering the faithful for religious services. He was teacher, doctor, even undertaker when family members and friends refused to bury their dead because of the risk of getting smallpox and other terrible diseases, the whiteman's unwanted gifts.

"Thank God, you have come, Bishop Grandin." The factor at Fort Carlton vigorously shook his hand. "One of my clerks has died of smallpox, another is sick. The Indians and Metis are dying everywhere. The clerk is a Protestant but he wants to speak with you. His minister has not come. Soon, I'm afraid, it will be too late. Will you see him?" The factor anxiously waited for his answer.

"Of course, of course. Where is he?"

"I will take you to him. But first, you must promise not to touch his hand. The disease spreads quickly from person to person. I am afraid to breathe the air in his room. You will not be disturbed if I do not go inside? Remember, don't touch him under any circumstances."

121

"If he offers his hand so I might console him, then I will touch him."

In a few minutes the bishop left the sick room, carefully closing the door. "He is resting. I don't hold much hope that he will get better. At least he's ready to die. Now where are the others?"

"The sick are mostly in the tents around the fort. The few who have escaped the smallpox are camped in the bush and open areas. They won't go near anyone with a fever."

Grandin walked from tent to tent, doing what he could to make the sick more comfortable. He had no medicine to fight the disease. It simply had to run its terrible and often deadly course. He heard the confessions of those who were dying, putting his head close to theirs to hear the final weak whispers of sorrow and repentance. Many asked him to baptize them before they died.

"An urgent letter for you, Bishop, from Father Lacombe." The factor caught up to Grandin when he stopped for a moment to rest. "He sent it by special messenger," he told the bishop between gulps of air to catch his breath.

Grandin ripped open the envelope to read the hastily written note. "I beg you to return to St. Albert immediately. Many are sick, including some of our priests and brothers. I am afraid we will all die, then there will be no one to minister to the sick. Please come."

The bishop folded the letter. "Father Lacombe wants me to hurry back to St. Albert. I must visit the rest of the sick here and gather more bodies for burial before I go." He left early the next morning.

The countryside was deceptively beautiful. Autumn sunshine flooded the plains and valleys; the last of the leaves fell gently with the tug of the brisk westerly wind. There was no hint that nature was ravaging the human population, forcing men and women to grab their children and flee in terror to escape each other.

The first indication that death was stalking the Indians and Metis came near St. Albert when he saw a young man run and stumble, then fall on the trail. "Everybody is dying.

Everybody is dying," he shouted, clutching a blanket in one hand and a piece of meat in the other.

Grandin covered the young man who now lay motionless in the grass, trying to comfort him, repeating what he had done for others on the brink of death so often in the past few weeks. The man died a few hours later. The bishop had no shovel to dig a grave, so he blessed the body and left it where it lay.

As Grandin tied his horse to the hitching post at the St. Albert mission, Lacombe appeared from around the corner of the house. Grandin read the strained and tired lines on his face.

"Come and rest for a few minutes. Then I will explain the situation." The two men sat at a table while one of the brothers made tea. "We are surviving here and those who are sick appear to be getting better but the disease still rages among the families in the settlement. Most of our priests and brothers are gone to help the sick and bury the dead in St. Paul and Lac Ste. Anne. The calls for help come from all over the diocese. People die so quickly we can't open enough graves. We are burying up to seven in each grave."

"I will start my visits to the St. Albert homes right away." The next morning Grandin took the Eucharist to the Cunninghams, the Belcourts, the Laderoutes and many other families along the Sturgeon.

During one of his visits a middle-aged man dropped to his knees at the bishop's feet, tears streaming down his cheeks. "Great priest of prayer, take pity on me. Pray for me. Six of my children have died. I have only one left. I am not angry with the Great Spirit. Pray to him. Beg him to leave this one who is sick to take care of me." Fortunately, the child lived.

The final death toll in St. Albert was three hundred out of a population of seven hundred people.

Just when the disease showed signs of subsiding, Grandin got an urgent message from Father Vital Fourmond, who was helping a roving band of Crees. "Come immediately. Smallpox is killing our hunters by the hundreds." At the height of the smallpox attack they were trying to hunt buffalo to stave off the threat of hunger in the desolate winter months just ahead. If the disease did not kill them, starvation would.

Grandin reined his horse to a halt at the outskirts of a camp on the grassland. A bedraggled group of men and women tottered and crawled toward him. Father Fourmond held the reins while the bishop moved among the sick. "We have lost so many of our best hunters. Almost all of the others are sick. These are the healthy ones. A visit from you will console them more than you can imagine."

"There is so much suffering everywhere I go. But here, it must be even worse to try to hunt when people are so sick and dying."

"Often there are not enough people with the strength to harness the horses," the priest replied. "You can't imagine how the sick suffer, jolting over the rough prairie, and how they feel when they see wild animals, lying there, waiting for their next victim to die."

The bishop moved from tent to tent without any concern for his own health. He had placed himself in God's care at Fort Carlton, again at St. Albert. There was no reason to think God would abandon him now. He tended the fires, cooked food, administered the sacraments and consoled the dying. The hideous sight of smallpox victims and the nauseating stench could not drive the missionaries away from the sick they were dedicated to serve. The next morning he celebrated an outdoor Mass to pray publicly for God's help. A devout group formed to follow him in procession from one teepee to another. He held the Eucharist high above his head to bless the sick and to beg the Good Spirit to rid them of the scourge that roamed unteathered throughout the West.

Eventually, as immunity built up in the tribes, the disease subsided, then disappeared. Before departing, smallpox left its mark on almost every family, claiming one-third of the people. The Indians and Metis remembered the devotedness and sacrifices of Grandin and his missionaries during one of the worst tragedies ever to strike them. As a result of the Oblates' heroism and devotion to the people, the Catholic faith grew rapidly.

The calamity in his own diocese should have been enough to keep Grandin occupied but he kept up with the news from Europe as best he could. Wars and uprisings rocked France and Europe. The Papal States were under attack from Italian nationalists. The events of 1870 so upset Grandin that he wrote to Pius IX, who was then presiding over the First Vatican Council, to renew his pledge of loyalty and friendship. All the priests and religious of his diocese signed the letter. Pius wrote back in thanks.

One happy event for Grandin in the midst of all the catastrophes was the marriage of Jean-Baptiste Pépin, his "little big vicar." The bishop was the celebrant at the wedding on an August day in Île à la Crosse. The bride's early life was a mystery. That her parents were dead was all anyone knew. Even her name has been lost. Grandin wrote enthusiastically about their marriage and his hope for their future. "Their education, their Christian preparation, everything was there to expect a model family. I am really pleased about it." Baptiste and his wife later moved to St. Albert and the young man continued his travels with the bishop.

"To the Pépin family," Grandin proposed a toast at a luncheon following the ceremony.

"To the Pépin family," the workers from the mission and their families replied.

Because there was only one way out of the remote settlement, Grandin travelled in the same caravan with the bride and groom. It was certainly the first time in Western Canada a bishop had travelled with a newly married couple on their honeymoon.

Albert Lacombe with Vital Grandin. (Courtesy Archives
Deschâtelets, Ottawa)

12

No Danger Too Great

"I SAW Natous throw back his blanket and grab his rifle. The shots and screams told the chief of the Blackfeet one thing. His most hated enemies, the Crees, were attacking under the cover of night. They wanted to kill his people asleep in their lodges."

Father Lacombe leaned forward, straining to remember every detail of his brush with death. "Natous screamed to wake the others in the camp before they were all killed. Bullets ripped through the teepees. I struggled to my feet in the darkness. The snow reflected just enough light so I could find my clothes. I put on my cassock, flipped the cord of my cross around my neck and prayed. How I prayed. I thought it was my last chance.

"'My God, I offer my life as a sacrifice for the conversion of your people, the Cree and the Blackfeet. Take my life if it will end the killing and bring them to you.'" Lacombe rocked slowly in his chair and drew on his pipe.

"Yes, yes, go on, Albert. What happened next? How were you injured?" Bishop Grandin leaned forward in his chair in the safety and warmth of the St. Albert mission. He wanted to hear every detail of his friend's near miss with death. "I will write Father Fabre later today. I don't think he has ever heard this story from your travels with the Indians. I must show the superior general the danger we face."

Lacombe reached for his cup to take a sip. Although the spectacular incident had happened three years before in 1865, Lacombe remembered every vivid detail. "I didn't know what to do. Flashes from the rifles came from all directions. Natous tried to rally the few men who weren't away hunting. I yelled to let them know a priest was there. You couldn't hear a thing for the war whoops and the screams of the wounded. I almost got trampled by the horses racing through the camp."

"I know what the noise is like. Even a friendly welcome with guns firing makes me deaf. An attack must be so much worse. But what happened then?"

"I rushed to help anyone I could. The wounded and the dying grabbed my hand. 'Have pity on us. Pray for us,' they begged me. A woman who had been shot in the head asked me to baptize her. She died before my eyes. A warrior burst into the teepee and scalped the dead woman. He grabbed the child at her side.

"I recognized some of the men as Assiniboines and Saulteaux, not just Crees. They destroyed twenty-five lodges and took everything of mine, including my breviary. Before I could do anything to stop the killing, one of the Blackfeet shot and scalped the attacker who had taken the breviary. It was horrible. He gave me my book back."

"What finally happened? How did the fighting stop?"

"Men came from two other Blackfeet camps to rescue us. But the fighting kept on until dawn. Finally, I made a flag, something to signal a truce. Then I started walking toward the Cree and the other attackers. Bullets whizzed past me. They didn't recognize me in all the smoke. The Blackfeet stopped but the Cree kept firing."

"Suddenly a ricocheting bullet glanced off my forehead and almost knocked me down. When the Blackfeet saw me stagger, they cried out to the others, 'Stop! Stop firing! You have killed the priest!' The battle ended, almost like magic. The attackers seemed embarrassed. 'We didn't know the priest was with you. We don't want to fight any more.' Many of them kissed my hand. They said I must be a god because the bullets had no effect on me. What do you think of that, Your Excellency?"

"Of course I am thankful you survived, but what about your belongings?"

"They apologized for attacking me. But I didn't get anything back, my clothes, my blankets, least of all my horse. In fact, I had to borrow some blankets. Finally, after six days of fighting through snowdrifts, we came to Rocky Mountain House. I was ready to collapse. I have never felt so tired and so poor in all my life."

Even the prospect of falling victim to the hit-and-run raids between warring tribes could not distract Grandin and his missionaries from moving freely among the Indians. They accepted the danger and the loss of their few possessions as part of the price they must pay. Grandin joined Lacombe and other priests to seek out the Plains Cree, living with them for months under the worst possible conditions — at least for someone raised in a European home. Just finding enough food was a daily gamble. On many days there was nothing to eat. Duck appeared on the menu most often with deer an infrequent delicacy. Buffalo was the Crees' mobile butcher shop. When the men slaughtered one, everyone feasted. Men and women would sit opposite each other in a semicircle for the evening meal. The approach was basic with no worry about table manners: one either used fingers and teeth as basic utensils or went hungry. When there was meat, an agile hand speared chunks from a boiling pot and served it without ceremony on a piece of wood.

While the approach to eating lacked a certain delicacy, if one could speak Cree there was a treat waiting, once the food was finished. The table talk intrigued Grandin. "Then the speeches began and the pipe was again passed around. These Cree speak with such ease and elegance that, were they in Europe, everyone of them would be a lawyer." He and the priests used the after-dinner discussion periods to teach the Indians about the whiteman's religion. The missionaries spoke of God, of his goodness and love, of sin, of heaven and hell. The Indians learned prayers and how the sacraments, baptism, confession and the Eucharist, could strengthen their lives.

The missionaries understood Indian life. They knew the Christian faith would flourish only if it took hold both at the grassroots and through acceptance by the chiefs. The progress they made with the obstinate Crees amazed Grandin. Already in the early 1870s he counted five hundred Christian believers among the adults and children.

The eagerness of the Indians to learn every detail of the new religion surprised Lacombe. "I was opening my mail in front of a group of the Crees and their great chief, Sweetgrass. One letter was from the Pope calling the First Vatican Council (1869-70)."

"The paper you are reading must bring you good news because you are so happy," the chief told him.

"The great master of prayer calls on all of the other masters of prayer to gather around him."

"Am I worthy to pronounce the name of the great prayer master?"

"Yes, you are a catechumen, on your way to baptism. You will all be sons of Pius IX before long," the priest told him.

"Would you tell us his name so that we may learn it?"

"Pius the Ninth. Pius the Ninth," Lacombe kept repeating the Pope's name.

Softly, Sweetgrass repeated the name several times as the priest said it, "Pius the Ninth. Pius the Ninth." Then the chief turned to his people. He seemed almost hypnotized. He called out in a loud voice, "Pius the Ninth. Pius the Ninth."

"Stand up," Sweetgrass ordered his people. "Say the great prayer master's name." The Indians rose to their feet. Once they were ready, he solemnly intoned the Pope's name, "Pius the Ninth."

They joined in a chorus never before heard on the plains, "Pius the Ninth."

As the last echo faded, the old chief asked, "Allow me to see the Pope's mark on the paper." He reverently kissed it. One by one the Indians followed his example. The incident so moved Lacombe that he often repeated it to Grandin and other Oblates. When he told the story Lacombe usually added the comment, "I wept as I saw how the great name of our common father so deeply touched the hearts and minds of our Indians. I could not help but think it might be some compensation for the blasphemies to which the revered name is subjected among the nations which claim to be civilized."

Sweetgrass became a strong Christian who tried to bridge the gulf between his people and the whites. When some of his people resisted the signing of Treaty Six in 1876 for central Saskatchewan and Alberta, he spoke so persuasively about the need to work with the whites that the other chiefs changed their minds. Sweetgrass so delighted the government official that he presented the renowned chief with several gifts including a pistol. Unfortunately the gun resulted in his death. A few months after the signing, friends of Sweetgrass were admiring the pistol in his lodge. Someone accidentally fired it and killed one of the West's great leaders.

While Grandin saw a slow conversion taking place among the Indians, he feared his whole mission effort would flounder for lack of money to support the isolated outposts. By 1871, the situation was desperate. Having to cut back, he halted construction on the new St. Albert cathedral. He temporarily abandoned the mission at St. Paul in what is now eastern Alberta, telling his missionaries to shelve their expansion plans. Hunger was the insatiable monster that devoured his resources. The survivors of the 1870 smallpox epidemic straggled into Saint Albert, begging for food and shelter. Parents, with children in their arms, pleaded, "The disease killed my wife. Who will help me look after our children?" Even more pitiful were those with no parents.

"The number of orphans has grown so rapidly. They come out of every nook and cranny. Those poor little ones have a good appetite. Just think that an entire side of beef can disappear in eight to ten days," his diary recorded.

If the human misery was not enough, he had to cope with the uncertainty of leading a diocese which still lacked formal recognition from the Vatican. Communication was slow in the West, but the delay that already stretched to three years was undermining Grandin's plan to make the Church as much a part of the prairie life chain as the buffalo that roamed in thundering herds.

"If God wants our work to survive and grow, then it will. But I think he wants us to ask for help. What better way to go to him than through his mother," he told the priests and brothers. "Our people are not ready to give. They have nothing to offer that would help to support and sustain us. I think we should do two things. Ask my brother Jean, my sister Mélanie and many other relatives and friends in France to pray for us. The second thing: I will consecrate the diocese to Our Lady of Victories."

The mission bell called the people to meet in the unfinished cathedral. They climbed the hill to the mission, bracing themselves against the stinging north wind. Grandin had chosen the feast of the Immaculate Conception, December 8, 1871, to consecrate his diocese formally to Our Lady of Victories.

"Ave Mater... Hail, Mother." The hymn flowed out through the cracks between the wallboards and into the valley. The procession of priests and brothers moved slowly down the aisle of the cold cathedral. Little did Grandin realize that day he was officially bishop of St. Albert. The Vatican had approved the establishment of the diocese in September but word still had not reached him. St. Albert would formally celebrate the installation of its first bishop the following April.

"Oh Mary, you will not allow things to remain in this state. You strengthened and helped the apostles in their trials. You will do as much for us," he prayed before the altar. He closed his eyes and his head fell into his hands. He did not hear the coughs around him from the cold dry air. The agony of his torturous journeys flooded his mind. He plodded again, step by step, behind his dog team across the ice of Great Slave Lake. The wind sharpened the tiny ice crystals, one by one, before they attacked his face. Then he was in his worn and battered canoe. "Jean-Baptiste, look out! The rocks, ahead. There to the right. We're going to hit!" Grandin threw his weight heavily to one side. The canoe swerved and exploded into calmer water. "Thank God," the bishop murmured.

Father Hyppolite Leduc leaned over and put his hand on Grandin's arm. "What is it, Your Excellency? Is anything wrong?"

"I'm fine." He rose slowly from his knees, the pain of years etched in his face. "Mary, our Mother, I consecrate the diocese of St. Albert to you under your title Our Lady of Victories."

Although he could drive the memories from his mind, his body could not erase the marks of struggle. "My health is good but I notice I am getting old. That must make you laugh," he wrote in a letter home. "However, it is true. My eyes are not what they used to be. I cannot read or write in the candlelight without my glasses. My memory is fading. My legs are worse yet. Not long ago I could walk on snowshoes for a whole winter. Soon I won't be worth anything."

Forty-two years old, he should have been in his prime. But his hair had turned white. His body groaned, weakened by the years of struggle. Not allowing himself to become discouraged, he renewed his determination to work even harder. So many people now depended on the Oblates, St. Albert must not fail. He took official possession of the diocese on April 7, 1872.

With the diocese's foundation firmly laid, Grandin encouraged the priests, brothers and sisters to redouble their efforts to establish the Church among the scattered bands, the Metis and fur traders. They had to cover a huge territory stretching from the American border, to south of Lake Athabasca, east to Hudson Bay, and north to the Arctic Ocean. Their resources depended largely on the generosity of Grandin's family and friends in France. He decided to recognize the support they had given so freely by naming Abbé Sébaux the honorary vicar of St. Albert. "I give it to you as a small acknowledgment of my gratitude."

He wanted to name his brother Jean honorary vicar-general of the diocese but decided against it because of possible criticism for apppointing a member of his family. "It would be a purely honorary title which you surely deserve for all of the services you have rendered. It seems to me this wouldn't be the right thing to do coming from your brother. If I were the Pope, I wouldn't want you to be anyone other than the priest of Martigne." The post of vicar-general went to Father Lacombe. "Don't look at the work of God in the diocese of Saint Albert as my exclusive work," Grandin wrote him. "It is also yours. Ultimately, it is God's and we are his men."

The day after his installation as bishop of St. Albert, Grandin packed his saddlebags.

"Excellency, your horse is ready," a brother told him. "He is tied at the post outside. Are you leaving for a long trip?"

"First I will visit St. Joachim in Edmonton. From there I will make the rounds of the other missions. What I want to do most is to spend the summer with the Cree and the Blackfeet."

"We will pray for a safe journey."

"Pray for all our people. Disease is attacking the Indians again and the whiskey traders are hard at work. Anything to make money. And the violence. Can you imagine that a young man stabbed his wife while they were drinking? That's what civilization produces, Brother."

"Before you go, a rider came a few minutes ago. He brought word that a band of Cree are on their way to visit St. Albert. They want to see the cathedral. The Indians can't believe such a building is possible. They have been travelling for several days and they want to speak with you."

"Of course, Brother. I'll wait until they arrive. A bishop must be everything in the missions, even a tour guide. If they think the cathedral is a marvel now, just wait until we finish the construction and hang our new paintings."

When the Indians arrived, they set up their teepees near the church. They stood looking at the building, then walked around it, excited by its size, eighty feet long by thirty-two feet wide.

"Welcome, my brothers. Come into God's big lodge. The Great Spirit has been waiting for you. I'm anxious to speak with each one of you."

Grandin moved freely from one visitor to another, urging them to treat the cathedral with reverence, just as they would their own sacred places. When they had seen everything and run their fingers over the smooth wood, he finally told them he must leave to visit their brothers and sisters scattered throughout his huge territory.

His brown horse pranced nervously as Grandin put his foot in the stirrup and swung into the saddle. He pressed his heels against the horse's flanks and began to pick his way carefully down the hill to the Sturgeon River. "Easy boy," he cautioned the horse. "Not so anxious." The mission bell rang through the valley. He stopped to recite the Regina Coeli, the familiar noon prayer of the Easter season. "Queen of heaven, rejoice. Alleluia." Praying for his missionaries, he asked God to give perseverance to the new priests and brothers who had given up their homes and families to work without prospect of any reward in this life. "Rejoice and be glad, O Virgin Mother." He had much to rejoice about. Lacombe would soon travel to Eastern Canada to look for support for the missions. And Grandin knew the Blessed Mother could not ignore his prayers. More help than he had expected had come from the Vatican and friends in France.

He looked down the valley of the Sturgeon. Patches of snow still clung to the shady spots along the south bank of the river. The aspen and poplar trees were bare. The promise of spring showed where the sun warmed the earth — he spotted tiny shoots of green grass, coaxed to life. Even that promise could not numb the searing pain of his father's death. The news had reached him only a few days before. God was clipping his ties to the Old World. Just as the seed falls to the ground to produce new growth for the next season, Grandin knew he must use his parents' gift of faith as the foundation for his work. He would never stop praying for them but he must let them go. God would fill the void. "For the Lord is truly risen. Alleluia."

13

His People Threatened

THE MEN slowly paddled their canoe through the shallow water near the river bank. They were scouring the sand for a crude wooden cross other searchers had told them marked the grave of Brother Alexis Renard.

"There, over there," Brother Alexandre Lambert shouted. "The cross, there. Just a few more feet."

They spotted a mound of sand. The five men silently prayed it would be someone else's grave, wishing Alexis might still be alive or, at the worst, lost in the great Lac La Biche forest.

They hauled the canoe up the bank, unloaded their supplies and turned over the frail craft to drain the water that had seeped through a small tear. Two of the men began to dig and scrape away the sand from the mound at the foot of the cross. The other three stood watching. Only the banging of the shovels broke the stillness as they carefully removed the top layer of sand. Within a few minutes they had uncovered several bones in the makeshift grave. They examined each one, looking for the teeth marks of a cougar or a bear which might have surprised and killed the brother.

"Any sign of an attack?" one of the men asked.

"Not that I can see," Brother Lambert replied. "But look at the skull. See the crack. He must have been killed with the axe we found. It has dried blood on the blade."

The men still resisted the conclusion they had found all that remained of Brother Alexis, even though they knew it was true. "May the souls of the faithful departed through the mercy of God rest in peace," Lambert whispered. He blessed himself, then bent down to gather the bones for the sad trip home.

"Amen." The brief response was barely audible as a sudden whirlwind of sand snatched and muffled the words. Startled by the swirling gust, the men shielded their eyes to protect them from the tiny grains. Quickly tracing the sign of the cross, they stared at each other for a moment, then turned away from the open grave.

The five wanted to load their canoe and rush back to Lac La Biche to deliver the brother's remains to Father Hyppolite Leduc, but their work was not finished. They must still search the bank and work their way inland along the trail to find some trace of the missing orphan girl and Louis Lafrance, the Metis guide who had been with her and Brother Alexis when they had left Athabasca. The men checked the heavy bush along the trail but they found nothing that gave any real clue to the girl's fate (there is no record of her name). Although they eventually did find several burned bones, they could not identify them but it led to speculation that Alexis' killer had eaten part of his victim's body or that of the girl.

The news of Brother Alexis' brutal murder in July, 1875, stunned those who knew him as a valued worker in the missions. He had travelled often with Grandin. The bishop believed the brother had died in an effort to save the girl from being raped by the guide. For that reason Grandin considered

Alexis to be a martyr. "I kept his clothing and the hatchet as precious relics." Still unresolved was the mystery surrounding the fate of the girl and the guide. Most people believed the guide had killed Alexis and the girl. But where was he? The West was large but it was not easy to hide for a long time without someone spotting a wanted man.

Stories began to circulate of a ghost who crept around Indian camps at night. "We are afraid to go out after dark. Our dogs disappear," an old man of the Beaver tribe told Grandin. One night, when the full moon painted their camp in a white delicate light, one of the men decided to wait with a gun for the ghost. He had lost a dog, one of his best.

"Stop," he shouted as a shadow darted from one teepee to another. But the figure, ignoring the command, glided from night's black cover into the faint, flickering light of the campfire, then vanished. The man watched from his hiding place. He saw someone crouching, just barely visible. Suddenly, the figure stood, took a few steps, then disappeared. The man with the gun took careful aim at the far side of the teepee, not wanting to hit anyone asleep inside. His muscles tightened. Beads of perspiration dripped from his forehead. "Stop," he shouted again as the figure darted for the safety of the trees.

Bang. The shot was like an exclamation mark emphasizing the seriousness of the command.

A moan came from the darkness. The shadow had been hit and hurt. Men rushed out of the teepees, clutching their rifles. "What happened? Who are you shooting at?"

"It's the ghost, the brother's killer. The one who steals our food and kills our dogs. Let's chase him before he gets away."

The men found no trace of the figure in the tall grass around the camp. They were terrified to wander into the trees. As soon as it was daylight, several armed men resumed the search for the wounded man. They found the guide's body near the camp.

Violence, an unwanted travelling companion, often appeared on the trail in unsuspecting forms. The weather could be one of the missionaries' most treacherous enemies lying in wait for them. Intense fast-moving storms trapped unsuspecting travellers. One of the victims was Louis Dazé, a lay missionary who assisted the priests and brothers. He froze to death in November, 1874, during a hunting trip. A sudden blizzard had hidden all signs of the trail and scrambled his sense of direction as he wandered for five or six days searching for a haven from the storm. Like Brother Alexis, Dazé's death was another grim reminder of the uncertainty of life in the wilderness.

Two other disasters tested Grandin's faith. A midsummer hail storm broke a hundred and fifty panes of precious glass in the cathedral and other buildings at the St. Albert mission. More serious was the destruction of the promising grain crops in the nearby fields. The community depended on the annual crop for food during the winter. The farmers helplessly watched the hailstones pound the shoots into the soil. They looked to the mission to fill their near-empty grain bins. The Oblates and Grey Nuns were still struggling to care for the orphaned children from the smallpox epidemic. Now more children and old people knocked on Grandin's door. "Bishop, we are hungry. Can you feed us?" Grandin could not refuse them.

His generosity kept the door open but it was the Grey Nuns' ingenuity that put food into the hungry stomachs. They made a barley broth laced with potatoes, cabbage, turnips and, on rare occasions, meat. They even baked it into cakes called "galette" as dessert. The menu was boring but it chased away the hunger pains.

The Sisters of Charity, more commonly known as the Grey Nuns of Montreal, had been caring for the hungry and the homeless in the West since Septembre 24, 1859, when Sister Emery (Zoé Leblanc), Sister Adèle Lamy and Sister Alphonse (Marie Jacque) arrived at Lac Ste. Anne, forty miles west of Edmonton, to care for the sick and to open a school. They moved to the St. Albert mission in 1863 to establish a new school and hospital. An addition in 1870 to serve patients with smallpox and typhoid fever was the first hospital building in central Alberta. Their work grew so quickly that by 1894 they were looking for land in Edmonton to build the General Hospital. Wherever there were Oblate missions throughout the West, the Grey Nuns worked along with the priests and brothers. Their number grew from the original three to almost two hundred by 1978.

If food lineups were not enough to worry Grandin, his old enemy, fire, tried his patience once again. He wrote in a letter, December 14, 1876, "A few months ago a fire destroyed the mission buildings at St. Paul, with the result that we have no school or other establishment for the Indians there."

Some of the news was good during those years of painful growth. The test of the missionaries' efforts was the acceptance of the Christian faith by the Indian bands. During a four-month tour of his diocese in 1874, Grandin discovered all the Indians at Île à la Crosse had embraced the faith. Among those preparing for confirmation was his old opponent, the "Son of God," who had once persuaded many Indians to break with the missionaries — but all that was long forgotten. Grandin's diary tells the story. "All the Indians here are not only Catholics but most of them are exemplary Catholics. May God be praised." Such acceptance of the faith chased away the memories of a thousand shivering nights on the trail. They fired Grandin with the enthusiasm of a young priest, eager to visit every mission, no matter how remote and difficult to reach. But he payed dearly for every night he slept in damp clothes on wet grass, developing an ear infection which added intense pain to his other afflictions. This newest attack on his health was one more burden he carried without complaining.

He wrote to his brother Jean, "The fathers here insist I go to France to consult specialists but I do not know what to do. I am fully determined, cost what it may, to teach a last lesson to my missionaries and to my people by dying at my post. I am fully convinced my dying would be a boon to my diocese." But that last lesson he so desired to teach was still years away. His pleas that someone else could more effectively lead the pioneer diocese failed to convince Church authorities. Despite his list of ailments, they were confident he was the man to deal with the torrent of immigrants rushing into the West to grab the Canadian government's offer of rich prairie land. Each settler could get a hundred and sixty acres of free land to cultivate, a place to build a new home. Even more precious for many was the gift of freedom, an escape from

Europe's wars and a suffocating society of privilege for the few. "At last, my own stove to spit on" was the way some immigrants greeted their first experience as landowners.

But what would become of the Indians and Metis, the great hunters who had enjoyed the same precious gift of freedom for thousands of years? Grandin's brother bishops believed he was one of the few men who could save the native people from destruction as European technology destroyed the ancient Indian way of life.

"High Priest, tell us what we are to do," an old Cree called out to Grandin. "If you had come when I was a young man, you would have seen herds of buffalo in the open places on both sides of the North Saskatchewan River, so many they would have almost blocked your way. Now they are gone. Where?

"In all the marshes you crossed, you saw the work of the beavers. Where are they today? What has happened to them? I'm not afraid for myself. I'm not worried about where they throw my bones. But what about my children and their children?"

Grandin could not give the old man an answer that would satisfy him. No one could. The bishop felt tension growing in the native people as they watched the old ways die. The new farmers could not tolerate herds of buffalo trampling their crops. The result was that the Indian's main source of food, clothing and shelter became almost extinct. The federal government rushed the establishment of a new administration to serve the European immigrants. The newly formed North West Mounted Police established detachments at Fort MacLeod and Battleford. The force rounded up the whiskey traders, the horse thieves and other criminals who roamed at will. Grandin supported the new force, but the police also served a political role — to establish the presence and authority of the new federal government. The Indians signed seven treaties during the 1870s, forcing them to exchange their lands across what would become the three prairie provinces for reservations and other benefits that were supposed to maintain their way of life. Despite all the promises made by the government agents, the living conditions of the Indians got so bad some faced starvation in winter and many women and children had no clothes. Between 1870 and 1890 Grandin wrote a steady stream of letters to the prime minister and the lieutenant-governor of the Northwest Territories describing the starvation and pleading for help for the Indians. In a letter January 24, 1881, Grandin wrote to Prime Minister John A. Macdonald, "... It seems to me that at Ottawa no one has a just conception of the extreme misery of our Indians in the N.W.T., especially in winter. In summer they receive their pay, find ducks and wild fruits and can live after a fashion, but in the month of December... at our own establishment of St. Albert, since the beginning of the month we have not given less than sixty meals a month..."

The response was always the same. The federal government disclaimed any responsibility for Indians not covered by the treaties and would not consider agreements until land was needed for settlement.

Although Father Albert Lacombe had moved to Winnipeg in 1873 to work in Manitoba for seven years, he joined Grandin and other bishops in their effort to gain some justice for the Indians. In 1875 he wrote to Alexander Morris, the lieutenant-governor of the Northwest Territories, "Another cause of the demoralization of the Indians... and not the least seems to be in some districts a lack of honesty on the part of the government employees in their dealings with the Indians. The Indian's ignorance and lack of competence is used to fool him and to lie to him either through the treaties or in other Indian agency matters. Later on the Indians realize they have been fooled and then their discontentment knows no bound..." Lacombe urged the federal authorities to consider themselves as the guardian and protector of all Indians, and to gain their confidence before the arrival of the immigrants.

"As for myself, I think that too little is offered to the Indians in return for the ownership of their lands. By signing treaties with them we deprive them of their lands, of their hunting, of their rivers, of their lakes, and leave to them only reserves which very soon will be surrounded by white settlements and frequently be devoid of game."

Grandin wondered how long the Indians would endure such misery. Their freedom to roam was disappearing, traded for land on reservations as part of the treaties the government was persuading them to sign. Did the Indians understand how much their lives had changed under the powerful whites? He eased himself into a chair. The years of struggle had left him worn out. God had saved him from hunger and death on the trail, but his problems had been simple compared to the complex threat against the livelihood of the native people. Could Grandin change minds and hearts in Ottawa? Perhaps, but even God might find it difficult dealing with politicians determined to fill the empty lands with farms and ranches. So much to do, so many letters to write. He must not lose touch with his family and friends in Europe. Without them he could not carry on the work of his diocese. He wrote many letters during the 1870s and '80s to Prime Minister Sir John A. Macdonald and Lieutenant-Governor Morris, calling for government action to help the starving Indians.

During those years Grandin had to contend with his own declining health made worse by an accident on his July, 1877, return journey from a meeting on the Indian situation with Bishop Faraud in the North. The horses pulling his wagon stumbled and spilled him down a river bank. Grandin rolled over several times, then finally lay still. "I'm not hurt," he told the guide, "except for a pain in my wrist. We must hurry. I have a lot do in St. Albert."

He had been far more seriously injured than he would admit. The nagging pains in his ears and head grew worse. He needed medical attention, the kind of treatment he could get only in Europe. Father Hyppolite Leduc, one of the bishop's consultors, decided to act against Grandin's wishes. He sent a letter in 1877 to the priests and brothers throughout the diocese.

"The state of his Lordship's health is becoming worse. The terrible pains in his ears are move severe than ever. So far all the efforts of the doctors and of our good sisters have been unavailing, as have been our public and private prayers. His sufferings are excruciating... In spite of what he has to endure, he thinks of you and speaks of you even during the most cruel of his crises. It is unnecessary to add, that in spite of his pain, he continues to practise the most heroic virtues."

When the superior general learned of Grandin's condition, he ordered him to return immediately to France for medical attention. Even that was not enough to make him go. Only when the priests and brothers of the diocese begged him to follow the superior's order, did he agree. Afraid he might never see St. Albert again, Grandin put the diocese under Leduc's direction and prepared for the long trip home to France.

Diocesan celebration at St. Albert. Bishop Grandin is in the center of the picture; on the hill behind are the St. Albert mission buildings. Left: residence for priests and seminarians (built 1879), later Grey Nuns' convent and boarding school. Center, second cathedral (1869-72); to its right, public school (1881-86); orphanage (1862-64), later serving as a hospital and then as a refuge during the Riel Rebellion. Far right: bishop's residence (1882-87). (Courtesy Archives Deschâtelets, Ottawa)

14

Slow Martyrdom

GRANDIN relaxed in a chair on the deck, his legs stretched out with a blanket to protect him from the blustery Atlantic breeze. He kept his coat collar up, with a scarf protecting his throbbing ears, and watched the green waves race each other in a contest they could not win. He breathed the salt air deeply, the smell of the ocean a tonic to rebuild his strength from the tiring trip from St. Albert to Montreal to meet his many good friends. His niece, Sister Marie Heurtebise Grandin, a daughter of Grandin's sister Anne, brought him special joy. She had joined the Grey Nuns to devote her life to her uncle's missions. She would help him bear the suffering of his final years.

The problems of the struggling diocese crowded out the worry over his illness. Once the West had been largely a French-speaking territory. Now with the arrival of so many immigrants from Britain and countries other than France, the French language was in danger. Grandin must find more French-speaking settlers, otherwise his missionaries and the communities they served would be isolated in a country that spoke mostly English, opening the way even more for Anglican and Protestant missionaries. Still unresolved was the disturbing problem of some factors at the Hudson's Bay forts. In the past they had offered hospitality to the Oblate missionaries, even chapel space. Now some closed their doors to the wandering priests.

A whole new set of complex problems had arrived on his desk as the Canadian Pacific pushed its tracks westward. Not only the symbol of the white advance, the railway was also the means. The Blackfeet threatened to block all railroad construction on their reserve. Any slowdown of settlement could only be temporary. New communities like Calgary and Fort Macleod were evidence of the development to come.

Even more painful was the continuing dispute with Bishop Faraud of Athabasca-Mackenzie over the control of the Lac La Biche mission. To settle the argument, Bishop Taché as mediator had decided Faraud should handle the material affairs of Lac La Biche, Grandin the spiritual. Instead of amicably settling the dispute, the agreement simply led to more bitter disagreements over its interpretation. The bishops could not decide the details of who should pay for what. Finances were always a serious problem in an area so large and so poor. The missionaries could not expect the Indians to support them through traditional offerings. As a result, the missionaries often went hungry. Giving was a complex reality in the native community. When gifts were given, larger ones were expected in return. Grandin relied on independent funds to buy the staples for his missionaries and the many others who depended on him. He received some support from the Congregation for the Propagation of the Faith in Rome as well as from his relatives and friends but it was never enough.

"Pardon, Your Excellency. May I remind you that we dock in Le Harve tomorrow?" a steward told him. "I must have your luggage early in the morning so it can be unloaded without delay."

Grandin looked up. "That will be no problem," he said with a smile. "I travel light this way. The return trip to Canada takes time to organize because of what I get from a lot of begging and a little buying."

Within a few days Grandin was a patient at the Lariboissière Hospital in Paris. "My dear Bishop, you have meningitis on both sides," a specialist advised him. "The treatment is simple. Avoid the cold at all costs. I know you live in Canada but there is nothing more I can tell you."

Grandin consulted another physician for a second opinion. His treatment involved air being blown into Grandin's ears and through his nose. While the doctor believed his patient's hearing had improved, the bishop was unconvinced. The treatment increased the pain and cost more than he was willing to pay. "I must leave to earn my living," he told the doctor, hurrying away to fill the many requests to preach to the French about life in his missions. His first stop was the famous church of the Madeleine in Paris.

He had to be careful. The Vatican Congregation for the Propagation of the Faith, the major Roman Catholic organization for funding mission work, had warned Grandin not to collect money during his preaching tours. Otherwise, the congregation would reduce the funds he normally received for his St. Albert diocese. He tried to bypass the powerful organization by appealing directly to the Pope and to the many other influential people he knew.

Pius IX had told him, "Organize an association to help your work and I will approve it." But before Grandin could get formal approval, Pius IX died. Church officials were mixed in their enthusiasm for an association, but Grandin kept trying to win support. While in Europe, Grandin decided to present his plan to the new Pope. Leo XIII agreed — the recommendations of other Church officials were enough to win his approval. "How can I say no when such an organization will raise money to support Catholic schools in the great

149

Northwest? As soon as it's established you will have my signature." Grandin was delighted. At last, money to build schools that would teach his Indians to live and survive in a whiteman's land.

"I have one more favor, Holy Father."

"Anything you wish. Within reason, of course."

"I have these pictures of you. Would you sign them so that I can give them to our missionaries as a souvenir of my trip?"

"At once. I will sign them this moment." Leo XIII disappeared into his office. A moment later Grandin heard an urgent call. "Your Excellency, quickly, I have had an accident."

Grandin hurried into the room. He found the Pope looking embarrassed. "Can you believe it?" he said. "Instead of using powder to dry the ink, I grabbed the inkwell and dumped some on the pictures. I'm afraid they are ruined."

Grandin did not mind. He was happy to leave Rome with the Pope's permission to form his society. What he did not realize was that the Propagation of the Faith had no intention of immediately endorsing the Pope's acceptance of a new society. No formal papal permission, no co-operation. Until it had the Pope's signature, Propagation would do everything to prevent Grandin from starting a rival organization to drain away funds. Its officials did not mince words. "No public collections. If you do, we will discontinue our support of your diocese."

Grandin was devastated. He pleaded with the president and directors of the organization. "My work is very different from yours. It couldn't possibly compete with you. The Pope approves it. So do many cardinals and the prefect of the Propagation." Grandin learned his main opponent was the organization's treasurer.

Surely the treasurer could not ignore a personal plea. The bishop had usually found quick acceptance of his requests and a generous response from those who met him and heard him speak. In this case, Grandin endured insults and the worst snub of his life.

"The treasurer scolded me very strongly for trying to find the help the Propagation of the Faith couldn't give me. In spite of my fifteen or twenty years as a bishop, I am almost treated as a school boy who has been caught doing wrong by his teacher." Grandin knew when to back off. He must keep the support of Propagation. His dream of schools would have to wait. If God wanted them, God would provide.

School bells of a sort already were ringing in the missions of the St. Albert diocese. Each missionary tried to provide some instruction in the three R's but few had enough time for the job. Grandin had established five larger schools, including three boarding institutions under the direction of the Grey Nuns. The bishop and his priests agreed that residential schools seemed the one hope for the Indians. By bringing the children together for instruction, the missionaries could teach them the whiteman's languages and how to live in the new and strange society as farmers and ranchers. The old days of hunting and fishing were dying. Little could be done for older Indians trapped in the past. The priests hoped the children would be the foundation of their people's future. Grandin revealed his foreboding in an 1881 letter to another of the missionary bishops. "Like you, I think that the Indians are bound to disappear. But I would like to send them into paradise." For Grandin, that required acceptance of Jesus Christ and his Church, the first objective of his mission among the Indians.

However, he was deeply concerned with the survival of the Indians as individuals and as a people. For him, the only way to do this was to make them French. He described the process in his writings when he talked about travelling with a young Indian he had known for a long time. "One of them, whom I consider more as a son because I rescued him from poverty and brought him up, is called after a bishop I revere. He is called Sébaux — thus we turn Indians into French people even through their names."

Grandin's loyalty to the Indians never wavered. He believed his education plan was the only option open to them. Without it they would surely disappear from the West. The Canadian government offered to pay half the cost of teachers' salaries but much more was needed. Where would he find teachers?

He persuaded a French congregation of sisters, the Faithful Companions of Jesus whose mother house was in Ste. Anne d'Auray, France, to work in the diocese after several refusals by English-speaking congregations to establish boarding schools for girls and high schools in Prince Albert, Calgary and Edmonton. "You ask me for a sacrifice, Your Excellency. Well, we shall make one for God," was the response of Mother Josephine Petit, the superior general of the Faithful Companions in 1883.

While the Propagation had refused permission for Grandin to establish his own mission society, many of his French compatriots and other Europeans pledged their support. As the French learned of his exploits in that land of mystery and romance, they considered him to be a hero, not only an outstanding Church figure but a Frenchman worthy of their highest esteem. As a result, his brother Jean collected thousands of francs for Grandin's missions. One incident embarrassed Grandin but it shows how much the French people loved and revered the "Indian bishop." He had just finished confirming eight hundred children in the church of St. Léonard in Alençon province, the final ceremony during a three-week visit to the diocese of Seez. The vicar-general, whom we know only as Canon Labreton, heaped praise on the bishop for his life of dedication to the Indians. Everyone in the crowded church stared at Grandin as the canon continued. The bishop began to fidget. He wished the vicar-general would talk about someone else. Beads of sweat formed under his miter. It felt like a steel band around his head, growing tighter by the minute. Suddenly his back stiffened. "No, he can't mean it," he said in a low voice. "Kiss my feet? Surely not."

"My Lord Bishop, you see these priests around you. We beg to kiss your feet which have carried the good tidings of the Gospel over snow and ice and endless prairies. These feet have grown so tired that now they can hardly carry your worn-out body."

Grandin could hardly refuse. The canon had asked him to give public proof of his humility. He nodded and took off his shoes. The thirty priests, including his brother Jean, came forward one by one, knelt and kissed his feet. Grandin squirmed and grew red at the display of affection. At one point a woman cried out, "How I would thank God if my son became a missionary."

As his popularity grew, partly through French newspaper stories of his adventures, he received many invitations to speak to gatherings. He was uncomfortable when those invitations took him into the salons of the wealthy and leaders of French society. His message of poverty and sacrifice was in stark contrast to the lives of those who spoke so admiringly of him. While they were not ready to alter seriously their own lifestyle, they were eager to see and hear a man who had left all to serve the Indians with heroic dedication.

Grandin's talks were simple and direct. His listeners appreciated his sincerity. Though certainly not famous for his one-liners, when the occasion was right Grandin could flash a quick wit. During a meal with a journalist, the man jokingly asked, "What is the difference between Grandin and 'gredin' (French for scoundrel)?"

Grandin looked up from his plate, paused for a moment and smiled. "My friend, it could be as little as the width of the table."

"Touché," the man groaned and broke into laughter.

Speeches in the salons of Paris gave Grandin a chance to contact people who were fascinated by stories of the untamed frontiers of North America, people who were captivated by his simplicity and who could generously support his work. He spoke eloquently of the hardships faced by his missionaries, how they willingly sacrificed everything, including their lives.

"We may well die of starvation and cold. We are not fortunate enough to die a martyr's death. Our poor missions are not so poetical. Our life is a long martyrdom, known only to God." That was his constant and unvarnished message. Rather than frighten people away, he attracted them. Young seminarians volunteered to work in his diocese, just as he had done years before when Taché had fired his soul as a young student preparing for the priesthood.

As much as he needed missionaries to serve the Indians and the new settlers, he was always careful in his selection of future priests. The thrill of the unknown often overshadowed the constant sacrifice the mission life demanded of young men eager for adventure. Grandin wanted no misunderstandings. They must be sure of their vocations to serve God in a special way. Of course, added adventure was a plus for those willing to trade the comforts of late nineteenth century France for the rigors of the frontier.

"If you should decide to come, let it be for God and only for God. Wait only on God for your reward. I would rather leave some Christian communities without a priest than give them a doubtful one. You see I make myself very clear."

Events quickly showed how timely his warning to the seminarians in Europe had been about the dangers in the missions. Soon after his return he faced the anguish of burying two young priests, a brother and another religious within eighteen months. Three of the missionaries had drowned in a boating accident, while one of the priests had frozen to death.

Grandin relied on priests and brothers from France but he dreamed of developing a native clergy. One of his most important decisions was to establish minor and major seminaries in St. Albert to train the local boys with the desire and the courage to become priests. When he left for Europe in late 1877 there were only four students in the seminaries under the direction of his nephew, Henri Grandin, his brother Florent's son. Late in his life, the bishop saw the beginning of his dream when he ordained Father Edward Cunningham in 1890, the first Metis to become an Oblate, followed by Father Patrick Beaudry in 1901.

After two years in France, Grandin decided he must return to his diocese. The treatments had failed to cure his earaches. "Why go to Paris to have someone blow into your ears?" was his feeling about the whole experience with the seven doctors who had tried to give him at least some relief. During the long gruelling return journey to St. Albert he made a decision about his future.

"God gave me a mission in a cold country... I would rather die twenty years sooner and die at my post than abandon my missions to live longer."

The horses strained in their harness, pulling two buggies along the frozen ruts of the narrow trail. The sun hung low in the sky, spreading a warmth Grandin rarely expected in late November. When the buggy, loaned to him by an old friend, reached the south hill overlooking the Sturgeon River, rifle shots and the booming of a cannon broke the stillness of the fall afternoon. Men on horseback circled the buggies. Father Leduc, who had represented the St. Albert Oblates at the congregation's general chapter in France, plus several new missionaries from Quebec marvelled at the welcome. The riders led the way to Father Lacombe's bridge. As Grandin stepped from the buggy, his priests and brothers, dressed in black cassocks and white surplices, knelt for his blessing. The Metis and other residents followed their lead.

"*Benedicat vos, omnipotens Deus...*" Grandin's voice flowed across the bowed heads in the sudden silence, "May almighty God bless you..." In the background the mission bell sounded a greeting. The speeches finished, he dressed in his gold vestments with his episcopal staff in hand and took the place of honor under a canopy for the final procession. Halfway up the hill it passed under a welcoming arch. Rifles and cannon again cracked and boomed. As the procession turned into the mission yard, heading toward the small cathedral, he was amazed to see a new white residence. How good God was to provide this new shelter from the winter's cold and summers' heat and rain. His own problems faded with the excitement of the homecoming. He realized his struggling church was growing.

"I am here to live and die with you," he told his people in emotional thanks for their welcome. "Thank God I am home." Many reached out to grasp his hand. Later that evening the pain in his head grew intense. Finally an absess burst, relieving the pressure. He would need every bit of strength he could muster to face new tests that awaited him.

15

Duelling with Old Tomorrow

"**N**O, PRIME MINISTER, I do not want industrial schools for our Indians run by people, people your minister will appoint. We are not trying to make gentlemen out of the Indians and Metis. We want them to become Christians. That is a job for priests and religious, not for civil servants."

"But surely, Bishop Grandin, the idea must have some merit. Such schools are working in France, I understand, with some success. After all, you were born in France. You must have some sympathy for, may I say, the French way of educating students."

Sir John A. Macdonald's smile broadened as Grandin's anger smoldered. For more than an hour he had tried to persuade Macdonald to establish Indian residential schools at St. Albert, Lac La Biche and Île à la Crosse. The prime minister had his own plan to build two schools, one at Battleford for Protestants, the second for Catholics at a site still to be chosen.

Macdonald tilted back in his creaky chair, his hands clasped behind his head. Grandin shifted uneasily in his straight-back chair. Long letters had not worked, a face-to-face meeting might. He had taken the initiative and travelled to Ottawa in 1882 to lay before the prime minister the serious problems faced by the Indians and the missionaries. Grandin wanted to show Macdonald how his civil servants were frustrating the missionaries' efforts to prepare the native peoples to cope with their new life.

He carefully listed many of the unfair situations imposed by the federal agents. "Prime Minister, we are wasting time. Your men in the West are persecuting my missionaries and my people."

"An extremely serious charge, Your Excellency. Can you prove your allegations?"

Grandin slumped forward. Macdonald watched as the bishop's head, crowned with a shock of white hair, slowly bowed. Then Grandin straightened, his back suddenly rigid, and began in a calm, deliberate voice. "Prime Minister, you challenge me to prove my statement that your men are persecuting us. I know I cannot do it to your satisfaction."

Macdonald's chair rocked slowly with a squeak that underlined the long silence. He wore a self-contented look.

"Let me tell you what is happening. Then you be the judge of your men's actions. In my diocese of St. Albert, most of the Indian children are Roman Catholics. But the men who run the reserves and make critical decisions for the Indians are mostly Protestants. Many of the instructors in the reserve schools are Protestants. The ministers of other denominations are allowed to build schools next to Catholic schools but the reverse is never allowed. Even though our schools are crowded we have little money to pay the teachers. The schools run by the other churches are all but empty. They have more than enough money to pay their teachers. What's more, you crowd the Indians on small reserves and order them to remain close to those reserves. It is impossible to assemble them for large gatherings."

"Now, now, Bishop Grandin, you can't blame the government for everything. The Indians agreed to the treaties. They accepted the conditions. Why, you and your priests were their advisers. Surely you must bear some of the responsibility. Give it time to work. The West is brand new."

"Prime Minister, my people were encouraged to slaughter the buffalo, now they are starving. If you continue to anger them, you will cause many more deaths."

Grandin expected to get little from the man whom political opponents called "Old Tomorrow" because he made promises but offered no timetable for keeping them. As part of the prime minister's delaying tactics, government officials cleverly used a list of grievances submitted by Grandin to establish an investigation that resolved nothing.

"I understand your concerns about education for your people and your need to have title to the land around your missions. I shall take them to my Cabinet. Good day, Bishop Grandin," Macdonald said brusquely, rising to his feet. The meeting was over.

Grandin spent five months in Ottawa lobbying everyone with power he could corner. His diary shows how hard he worked.

"Feb. 14. I spent part of the morning at the Parliament. I saw different ministers, senators, elected representatives. I returned a little tired."

"March 3. I am going to see the custom's minister... Upon his advice we went to see the minister of finance... I learned that the minister of the interior has put my case into the hands of Mr. Edgar Dewdney (the Indian commissioner and lieutenant-governor for the Northwest Territories)."

While Grandin received much encouragement and pledges of support, he needed written confirmation from the prime minister that at least some of the demands would be fulfilled. The inevitable delays made him impatient. "Sorry, but Sir John can do nothing until the session ends." Grandin pursued the politicians as doggedly as they adeptly concocted excuses for their lack of action. The Montreal newspaper *L'Étendard* applauded Grandin's years of sacrifice under the most horrendous living conditions. Calling him "a new hero," the newspaper urged the federal government to act on the bishop's requests. "Moreover, if their hearts are really set on a fast and safe settlement of the Northwest and if they do not want to make it necessary for them to exterminate the Indians, as our neighbors do (referring to Indian wars in the United States), they could not be better advised than to favor the Roman Catholic missions."

Finally, word came from the prime minister's office. There would be some concessions. For Grandin it was like finding a cache of pemmican on the prairie. A small cache was better than an empty hole. He left Ottawa with the land titles to all of the mission properties in his diocese, and the territorial government would appoint a paid bilingual magistrate. These were small victories when one considered that Macdonald had refused to contribute any funds to the operational expenses of the children's homes Grandin operated. The prime minister rejected Grandin's plan for three industrial schools, and instead would proceed with his own plan to build one school for Catholic and one for Protestant students. The school battle was far from over.

Grandin had learned the power of publicity and how quickly politicians respond to issues that arouse voters. He realized too that his people did not appreciate the importance of Christian education. Given the choice, many would choose a public school education in order to learn English and something about business. However, the bishop refused to give up hope. One valuable lesson he had learned during his years of struggle against the fierce northern climate was the need to keep some food for extra days on the trail. Father Albert Lacombe was his secret weapon in the school fight, the perfect man to take over the political battle.

"Don't forget, you have to keep bothering these gentlemen of the government to get something from them. Tell them, if they try to make fun of you like they did of me, I shall return to Ottawa. I won't let them rest until they do something."

Grandin took home another partial victory. Because the bishops of Canada feared a new mission association might weaken support for other causes, they voted against his request to form an organization to support his schools.

Instead, they approved an annual collection. The collection had some advantages. It gave Grandin the chance to gain national exposure for his diocese. The bishops urged him to write a pastoral letter to appeal not only for funds but for young men to become Oblate lay brothers.

He wrote in his first pastoral letter in 1883, "Our brothers are missionaries, humble and hidden missionaries, it is true. But nevertheless they are real missionaries, who in their sphere co-operate with the priests in advancing civilization and in extending the reign of Christ.

"Some of them are expert carpenters, others are qualified mechanics, tailors, farmers, cobblers and so on. All of them work hard and faithfully, but like the priests and bishops they work not for earthly gain but exclusively for the glory of God and the salvation of souls."

His national campaign launched, Grandin headed back to St. Albert in 1883 with three new priests, two lay brothers, four young men interested in becoming missionaries, and eight sisters (members of the Faithful Companions of Jesus) to work in new boarding schools for girls. The diocese needed every worker the bishop could recruit. Twenty-five parishes and missions now served the Indians and Metis and the thousands of new settlers.

The Canadian Pacific Railway was quickly pushing westward, not only making transportation faster across the huge country but also changing life on the prairies. The last spike in the transcontinental line would be driven in 1885. The arrival of trainloads of immigrants strained Grandin's limited resources. The new communities needed churches and priests who could speak their languages, as well as schools. He resolved to fight stubbornly for the Church's right to establish schools. Despite the guarantees of religious education and language rights passed in 1875 by the Canadian Parliament and handed over to the territorial councillors to administer, he was cautious, always on guard. His persistence helped Catholic parents to carry those rights into Confederation when Alberta and Saskatchewan became provinces in 1905.

Settled again into life in St. Albert, he faced another ordeal. September 15, 1884, the bells of his cathedral and the convent suddenly burst into enthusiastic song, breaking the calm of the September morning. Such activity usually had one of two meanings. The community was in danger or there was a special occasion to celebrate. As he climbed the steps of the porch to the mission house, Grandin heard the steady drone of conversation through an open window. Missionaries who saw each other only on rare occasions were trading stories about life in the bush. The voices stopped as he appeared and the forty priests and brothers dropped to their knees. Only the quiet sound of two moths excitedly attacking a lamp glass relieved the muggy silence inside the room. Outside, the bells called all within their sound to celebrate Grandin's twenty-five years as a bishop. The sight of his fellow priests and friends all kneeling before him embarrassed him. He quickly motioned for them to sit down.

Father Leduc was the first to speak. "This feast day is our own joy, our own glory. The glory of the father is so well reflected on his sons. Your Excellency, we offer you our hearts with all the love they are capable of. We bring to your feet our most absolute dedication to the work that has been entrusted to you and which is God's work par excellence. We present to you the offering we have collected from our relatives, benefactors and friends."

The speaker led the bishop into the cathedral. Laid out on the altar were new Mass vestments, a monstrance to hold the Eucharist during Benediction, and other gifts for the celebration of the liturgy. Two wooden angels carved by Brother Patrick Bowes decorated the sanctuary. Grandin gratefully accepted a chalice and a missal from Oblates throughout the world. "I am deeply touched." He looked through tears from one blurred figure to another, men and women who shared his work. His greatest joy was that his missionaries were loyal to their calling and to him. Even more important than the celebration of his anniversary was the public recognition of his confreres' perseverance, unshakable in the face of hunger, cold and the clouds of mosquitos that drove men and animals to the edge of madness. He gave those around him the credit.

"If I have done a little good, it was not by myself... In this country we often travel on sleds pulled by dogs. The lead dog is the most highly valued because it is the one that guides and leads the others. It is not the best one, the one that works the hardest or tires itself out pulling the most. Those that follow do the work and have the trouble.

"Well, I am the head of this diocese. I am the honored one today. But these honors belong to others as well. They must be showered on them much more than on my unworthy person."

Despite his attempts to deflect the tributes, Grandin could not escape. People came from Edmonton and many isolated missions to honor him. Anglican missionaries offered their congratulations in a gesture of good will that helped ease the tension and drain some of the bitterness that had existed for decades between the two denominations. Painful as he found it to be regarded as a hero, Grandin accepted the celebrations as a way to strengthen the Christian community. He wrote in his diary, "The main thing is that all this be used for the glory of God."

The celebration of his twenty-five years as a Western bishop served as a moment for the Oblate missionaries and their bishop to pause and enjoy their triumphs. Hidden within the glare of the public recognition of their successes was the nagging uncertainty over the future of the Indians and Metis. Indian leaders, such as Crowfoot of the Blackfeet in southern Alberta, bitterly resented the wounds inflicted by the whites on his people. When the train whistles of the Canadian Pacific Railway were just a few miles from their reserve at Gleichen, fifty miles east of Calgary, Crowfoot had sent word that the rail line must not cross the corner of his reserve. If it did, he was angry enough that he would order his people to massacre the construction workers.

Grandin had searched for someone to propose a compromise that would avoid bloodshed. That person was Father Lacombe, a man the Blackfeet trusted. Canadian Pacific officials did not want a confrontation with the Indians. For the Blackfeet, it was time to stand firm. Today it was the railway. What would be tomorrow's excuse for more land to be taken away?

The bishop hung on Lacombe's every word as he poured out the story about his dealings with Sir William Van Horne, the general manager of Canadian Pacific. "Getting Van Horne to agree wasn't hard. I used their telegraph to make my proposal. What a marvellous invention. They don't want to stop or even slow down construction for anything."

"But Crowfoot, how did you convince him to be reasonable?"

"As soon as Van Horne said yes, I bought two hundred pounds of sugar, the same amount of tea and tobacco and sacks of flour. I was ready. I sent word I wanted to speak to Crowfoot and his people."

As Lacombe described the 1883 meeting at Gleichen, Grandin could visualize the scene only too well. The great chief would arrive on horseback, the elders and warriors gathered in a circle around him, their horses pawing the ground, tails swishing to brush away the flies. So many times he had stood alone before Indian leaders in similar situations to urge them to reconsider their decisions. Grandin could almost recite word for word what Lacombe's message would be. But first, according to custom, the supplies must be distributed, then the priest could speak.

"I beg you to listen to me," Lacombe had pleaded with the Blackfeet. "If there is one individual among you who can say during the fifteen years I spent with you that I gave him bad advice, let him stand up and say it without fear." The priest looked first at Crowfoot, then from one elder to another. No one spoke.

"My friends, I have one piece of advice for you today. Let the whites move across your land and do the work to build their railway line. They cannot take the land away from you for ever."

Some of the Indians began to murmur. Crowfoot held up his hand. "Let the prayer chief speak. He is our friend. We must hear him."

"The whites who go across your land are workers. Your quarrel is with their leaders. You must settle the problem with them, not kill those who lay the tracks. I have told their leaders of your anger, that you are ready to fight to keep your land. They understand how much the land means to you. The lieutenant-governor has agreed to come in a few days to listen to your complaints. If you are not satisfied with his offer, you can still force the workers to leave."

The Indians hurriedly discussed his offer. Lacombe stood silently facing them, his black cassock blowing in the strong spring breeze. He had spoken to them as persuasively as he knew how, hoping to avoid a massacre. Now Crowfoot must decide whether to follow the priest's advice or to attack the construction crews.

Crowfoot raised his arm for silence and stood in front of Father Lacombe. "Prayer Chief, you have been our friend for a long time. We have listened to your wise advice. If we can be sure the railway will give us more land than what it takes to build the line, then we will not harm the workmen."

Grandin sat back in his chair, a smile under his eyes. "Père, that Crowfoot is a wiley leader. He knows that killing the construction crew won't solve anything. But what about the lieutenant-governor? Did Dewdney show up?"

"Edgar met with Crowfoot and his people within a few days. In trade for the railway land he promised to give the Blackfeet a hundred times as much land on the southern end of the reserve. If they didn't like what he offered, Dewdney said the construction work would end and the workers move off the reserve."

"Of course they accepted his offer."

"They could not refuse a land trade like that. The construction is underway again and will be well into the mountains by June."

Unfortunately, not all confrontations between the native people and the whites would be resolved so easily and without violence. The unsettled list of Metis land grievances led to secret meetings in remote cabins. The federal government outraged Metis landowners when it broke a promise that a special survey would leave their long, narrow farms intact. The people raised $600 to send Father Leduc and another delegate to Ottawa to persuade federal officials to reverse their decision. With Grandin's strong support for the St. Albert Metis, the government finally gave in.

Although the Metis won in the St. Albert district, they could not get ownership of their lands in other areas. Prime Minister Macdonald ignored warnings from the missionaries and even his own officials that frustration, if left to fester, could produce rebellion along the banks of the North and South Saskatchewan rivers. But "Old Tomorrow" would not be deterred from his game of power politics.

Grandin and his missionaries wanted to be peacemakers. They supported the demands of the Metis for a land settlement that would give them the security that comes with ownership. Frustration and anger mounted as the years edged closer to 1885. Grandin was convinced only large reserves could be adequate buffers between the Indians and the loose-living whites. At the same time, the Oblates urged the Metis and Indian leaders to restrain the extremists who insisted that Macdonald would listen only to the crack of the Winchester rifle.

16

No More Begging

WANDERING SPIRIT crouched on one knee in the main aisle of the small log church of Our Lady of Good Counsel in Frog Lake, now in Alberta on the Saskatchewan border north of Lloydminster. He leaned on his loaded Winchester, one finger gingerly stroking the trigger. The tall lithe Indian understood well the value of spreading terror as part of the prairie fighter's hit and run tactics. The war chief of the Plains Cree was dressed to kill. A lynx-skin war bonnet covered his thick black braids of curly hair, unusual for an Indian. Five eagle feathers, marks of battle, decorated the bonnet. Yellow war paint covered his eyelids, lips and chin. Wandering Spirit glared at Father Felix-Adélard Fafard. The pastor of Frog Lake was trying to ignore the threatening gestures and rising din as he celebrated Holy Thursday Mass, April 2, 1885.

The open rebellion feared by the missionaries was catching fire. The French Metis were fed up with Prime Minister Macdonald's political tricks to delay action on their demands for land scrip. Louis Riel, the Metis mystic and leader, refused to wait any longer. He declared his Provisional Government of the Saskatchewan, March 18, 1885, a break-away state similar to the one he had established fifteen years earlier in Manitoba. Gabriel Dumont, the king of the buffalo hunters and Riel's field commander, won the first battle, March 26, when his men killed a dozen policemen and volunteers at Duck Lake. Now Cree leaders saw a chance to regain their former freedom by joining the rebels.

"*Dominus vobiscum*," Father Fafard said as he turned before the terrified congregation. Surely the Lord was with these men and women, in the face of the simmering hatred of the Cree warriors.

"*Et cum spiritu tuo*," a lone voice replied bravely, "... and with your spirit too."

How Father Fafard prayed the spirit of the Lord would enter his every fiber that day, turning his weakness into strength. The French missionary was the only one with enough prestige to strip Wandering Spirit of his power. But how? Promises would not work any longer. Fafard feared one command from the war chief would be enough to unleash a massacre.

Young warriors wandered into the church, singing and dancing to the steady beat of a drum. They showed off the clothes and drank the liquor they had looted from the Hudson's Bay store and the settlers' homes. Fafard raised his hand to caution Father Félix Marchand, a young priest from the nearby Onion Lake mission, not to interfere. The warriors would shoot at the slightest threatening gesture. Without warning, the war chief pumped several shots over the heads of the priests as he prowled the main aisle of the church. Indians and whites hugged the floor. A window shattered and wood splinters showered those huddling for cover near the door.

"Our Lady of Good Counsel, save us," Father Marchand prayed over and over. He had brought his small congregation from Onion Lake to Frog Lake because he believed here they would be safe from attack. Fafard had worked among the Indians for ten years. He was a friend of Big Bear, the chief of the Crees. What the two priests did not know was that Big Bear had lost control of his warriors. Wandering Spirit, enflamed by the news of the Metis victory over the police at Duck Lake, a hundred and ninety miles east, convinced the young warriors to paint themselves for battle. He hated the whites for the treaties that forced him to trade the freedom of the bush and prairie for the confinement of the new reserves.

Father Fafard ended the Mass abruptly. If the other warriors started shooting at random, they could all be killed. Outside the church he might convince them to return peacefully to Big Bear's camp. The priest stood at the altar rail, quietly urging the Indians to leave. Wandering Spirit scowled when he heard the priest take charge. He would settle this outside.

"Go," he shouted to the congregation. "Go."

Indians and whites hurried outside the church. The priests slowly removed their vestments, stalling for time as they considered what they should do to calm the Indians and end the danger to the whites.

"Hurry," Little Bear yelled as the priests left the church.

"But I must lock the church."

Little Bear glared into the priest's face. He lunged at him with his rifle butt, striking Fafard under one eye. Blood spurted from the wound. Louis Goulet, a Metis, jumped on Little Bear. "Stop," the priest shouted. "They'll kill us all."

A few minutes later the group reached a house next to the police detachment. Wandering Spirit then ordered them to walk half a mile to Big Bear's camp, with the promise that none of the whites would be hurt. Tom Quinn, the federal Indian agent, refused.

"If you want to live, you'll go," threatened Wandering Spirit.

"I've had enough of you and your warriors. I won't move." Quinn did not like Indians, even though his mother was a Metis and he was married to a Cree. Wandering Spirit hated Quinn because he often refused to give the Indians food, unless they did extra work. They called him "The Man Who Always Says No," and "Sioux Speaker," because of his Indian ancestry.

"I've had enough of you," Wandering Spirit snarled. "I'm going to kill you." He fired one shot into Quinn's head, who fell dead at the war chief's feet. No one could stop the violence now. Wandering Spirit danced in the road around the agent's body, waving his rifle. "I have killed Sioux Speaker," he chanted.

"Kill, kill," the warriors screamed. The whites under guard in one of the houses stared at each other in disbelief. The worst had happened. Someone had lost in a deadly confrontation with Wandering Spirit. Mothers tried to hide their terrified children.

Outside, Big Bear realized his authority as chief of the Plains Cree had not only been challenged but would completely collapse if Quinn's death prompted more killings. He pushed and shoved his way through the dancing warriors who were working themselves into a frenzy from the effects of the whiskey and the sight of blood oozing from the agent's head wound.

He shouted for them to stop, trying to raise his voice above the shrill cries of the angry mob. Horses reared back, their hoofs beating out a tattoo against the chilling whoop of the Cree war chant. Above it all the voices of Wandering Spirit and Big Bear duelled for the warriors' attention.

"Kill, kill," screamed the warriors.

"Stop, stop," Big Bear shouted.

Volley after volley declared Wandering Spirit the winner of the deadly shouting match. When Father Fafard knelt to comfort John Delaney, one of the first to be hit, Bare Neck casually raised his rifle and shot the priest. Badly wounded, he was still alive and moaning. Walking the Sky, a young Cree whom Fafard had fed, clothed and received into the Church as a new Christian, raised his rifle and shot the priest in the head.

Marchand yelled in horror and rushed to the older priest's side. Wandering Spirit swung around, firing once. The young priest died instantly, his body pitched face first into the melting snow and mud. Fafard died soon after. Not all the Indians joined in the massacre. The killing of the nine whites upset many of the Crees but they were powerless to stop the looting and burning. The warriors drank the wine Father Fafard used for the celebration of Mass and paraded around the church in his vestments.

Three days later, on Easter Sunday, was the final act of desecration. The rampaging warriors threw the bodies of the two priests into the basement of the church and set it on fire. As the smoke rose over Frog Lake, the Indians shrank back in terror. An evil sign appeared in the sky. In the smoke from the burning logs and bodies they saw the form of a man and a horse. They interpreted it to mean that soon hundreds of whitemen on horses would take revenge for the killings.

News of the latest killings quickly travelled southwestward to Edmonton, adding to the tension already caused by the March 26 Metis victory at Duck Lake. The telegraph had tapped out that chilling report, then went dead. Edmontonians who met in general stores and saloons most often asked each other, "Will the Cree and Metis join the uprising?" The large community of Metis at St. Albert had been seen as no threat to Edmonton because many white residents were fighting their own land battles with the federal government. But the shocking news of the Frog Lake massacre and an April 3 raid by two Cree bands on a government storehouse at Saddle Lake near St. Paul threw Edmonton into panic. An emergency meeting at Kelley's Saloon worked out a defence plan. Residents strengthened the walls of old Fort Edmonton on the north bank of the North Saskatchewan River (today at 109 Street) to make it safe for the women and children.

Many others in the district decided it was better to take refuge at the St. Albert mission, convinced if anyone could save them it was Grandin. The bishop assured the refugees they would not be harmed. They filled the school, the workshops and every available space. "We have no ammunition and no guns. I am pleased about that. I hope this will be our salvation. Do not load your guns. If the Indians come,

I will go to meet them with two of the priests and a few Metis. We will do whatever we can to stop any blood from flowing."

While the residents still feared an attack, the confrontation came not at St. Albert but sixty miles south of Edmonton near Ponoka. Chief Ringing Sky and his warriors of the Bears Hills bands joined the revolt. They looted the Hudson's Bay Store and a farmhouse at Battle River Crossing. Before moving north April 12, to join Big Bear's force at Fort Pitt for an assault on the police and volunteers, they decided to hold a war dance. That delay was the opportunity Father Constantin Scollen, the Irish missionary of Bears Hills, needed to calm the excited warriors. Chief Ringing Sky was to learn how the bold action of one man could block their plan.

"Stop. Wait. You must listen to me before it's too late. Many of your young men will die." Father Scollen did not like being ignored. He walked right into the middle of the war dance, looking for someone who could persuade those he called "the young rascals" to listen. The warriors fired several shots over his head to frighten him but the priest refused to back away.

"Riel, Riel. No surrender," they screamed at Scollen.

One man did listen. The priest convinced Chief Bobtail that the Indians would lose far more than they could gain. The chief pushed through the dancing throng to silence the drums. In the confusion Scollen produced a weapon which the warriors, heavily armed with rifles, just could not match. He launched into a two-hour sermon that eventually broke up the gathering.

Fortunately the Blackfeet and other bands of the south did not join the rebellion, largely through the influence of Lacombe and Grandin. With fighting localized in the northern communities and through serious blunders in battle tactics by Riel and Dumont, the Metis leaders saw their dream dissolve in their defeat at Batoche in mid-May, 1885, by the forces of Major General Frederick Middleton.

As government officials prepared for Riel's trial in Regina and searched for the fleeing Dumont, Grandin began rebuilding his missions and healing the deep scars left on the people. The deaths of Fathers Fafard and Marchand and the wounding of Father Julien Moulin, parish priest at Batoche for thirty-two years, devastated the bishop. Once the fighting ended, he headed north to visit the missions and the scene of the massacre at Frog Lake. He broke into tears when he prayed over the priests' graves. At his request, the people erected a cross to mark the spot where the missionaries had died. "Since I returned from Europe, I have lost eight missionaries. Only two died in their beds. The others froze to death, drowned or were killed by the Indians," the bishop wrote in a long letter to Fafard's mother in France, describing how her son had died and the care with which an Indian woman had treated the bodies of the two slain priests. "I keep your worthy son's rosary for you."

Grandin faced a major rebuilding job in Frog Lake and seven other missions damaged or destroyed during the rebellion. He also faced a painful reconciliation with many Metis who believed the missionaries had betrayed them during the fighting. They had refused to support violence, but from the earliest rumblings of discontent the Oblates had supported the demands of the Metis for a fair land deal from the Canadian government. In his letters and discussions with government officials, Grandin had urged quick action to produce a just settlement. He set the tone in an 1884 letter to Public Works Minister Hector Langevin in an effort to head off violence.

"I deplore the way the government has of showing a real contempt for the country. The members of the government should not ignore that the Metis as well as the Indians have their national pride and get angry at the contempt of which they think they are victims. Once they have been pushed to the limit of their patience, neither the priests nor the bishop will be able to make them see sense. I therefore beseech you, Your Honor, to exercise all your influence so that their rightful demands will be taken into account."

Grandin understood the importance of land in the Metis claims. He had seen how the once self-sufficient Indians suffered from their dependence on white technology and the imitation of the worst features of white life. At least the Indians had their reserves, islands of land which were their own. There were no treaties for the Metis, the indispensable middlemen between the Indians and the whites. Without the Metis, the fur trade would never have been possible. Now the government ignored their need for a secure land base to make the switch from the dying fur trade to agriculture, the West's new economy. Riel had tried to right Metis grievances by building a new Christian city.

"Riel strikes me as a very excessive man in religion as well as in politics. I am afraid that he might become insane. Several of my priests and Metis share my fears. But the majority of the Metis consider him to be an oracle," Grandin had written in several letters to warn government officials of the danger in ignoring Metis demands.

Louis Riel had come into conflict with the missionaries for a combination of his political tactics and his religious aspirations. When Father Alexis André, the Oblate superior in the North, refused to approve Riel's formation of a provisional government, the Metis leader called him a traitor and accused the priests of abandoning the people. The gulf widened even more when Father Vital Fourmond advised the Metis during Sunday Mass in Batoche in March just before the rebellion began that the priests would refuse them the sacraments, if they took up arms against the authorities. The Oblates' hard line shocked the people. Opposition to violence was one thing, but how could the priests refuse the sacraments to nourish their souls?

After the Mass, Riel unleashed all his fury on Fourmond during an exchange in the Batoche churchyard. "You have turned the pulpit of truth into one of politics, falsehood and discord, in daring to refuse the sacraments to those who would take up arms in defence of their sacred rights," the Metis leader shouted.

To show his mission had the approval of the Church, Riel had produced three letters from Bishop Ignace Bourget of Montreal. Father Fourmond would not back down. "I've seen those before. They're old. They don't support what you claim. I have nothing more to say."

The silent crowd parted as the priest strode quickly toward the church door. The tassel on his biretta bobbed in the sharp March wind as he struggled to hold it on his head.

The Oblate cross, stuck at an angle in his sash, bobbed as he strode away.

Riel had turned in disgust. "Do not listen to this priest. Listen to me. I will explain what's happening." The knot of men and women tightened around him. Which one spoke the truth? Should they follow their priests or the man they called a prophet?

Riel, tall and intense, cast a striking figure standing in the snow. His language hypnotized the anxious crowd. "God's Spirit has fled from the Pope in Rome to engulf our friend Bishop Bourget in Montreal, the man who understands and supports our struggle for a new Christian city in this land. If our priests do not support our crusade, then we will ride into battle without them. If they will not administer the life-giving sacraments, then I will."

The split had widened further a few weeks later when Riel again angrily confronted the priests and led a group of supporters to occupy the Batoche parish church of St. Antoine de Padua. Incensed, Father Moulin called Riel a "heretic."

"Protestant," Riel shouted, laughing at the priest. As Moulin retreated, Riel cried out, "Rome has fallen."

Later, when Moulin had rejected Riel's invitation to become the first priest of a new religion, the Metis leader threatened to drive him from the West. Father Végreville's refusal to be the chaplain for the Metis forces further angered Riel. "Then I will be your priest," he told his people.

Riel believed his mission was to establish a new but stricter faith in the West. The Exovidat, the Metis ruling council, proclaimed it the "Living Catholic and Apostolic Vital Church of the New World." While its most fundamental changes were the eventual extinguishing of hell's fires and the replacement of the doctrine of the real presence of Christ in the Eucharist with a symbolic presence, Riel also adopted practices that affected the daily lives of the Metis. He gave religious names to the days of the week and moved the Christian day of worship to Saturday. Only one of the ten members on the council had failed to support a resolution officially designating Riel a prophet.

Some Metis now accused the Oblates of betraying the rebellion by giving General Middleton information about their numbers and supplies before the crucial battle at Batoche. The missionaries denied the charge, insisting they had honored their written pledge not to take sides.

The aftermath of the rebellion produced several contradictions. Once the fighting ended, Riel and the priests he had taken hostage in the rectory of St. Antoine were among the first to be reconciled. The bitter words hurled at each other by Riel and the missionaries in the churchyard exchanges in the tense days before the rebellion were forgiven and forgotten. Riel, whom the Oblates blamed for the violence, the "anti-Christ" who had tried to destroy the Church, withdrew his religious claims and died on the gallows with Father Alexis André at his side as his chaplain. This was the same Oblate superior who before the rebellion had urged Prime Minister Macdonald to buy off the Metis leader with $5,000 to return to the United States. Now André called Riel a "saint" while he awaited execution in his Regina cell.

Grandin could easily have been embittered by the death of his two priests and the destruction of eight missions. Few people would have disagreed with him if he had resigned his diocese and returned to France. Instead, he acted quickly to aid the victims, the hungry and homeless women and children whose husbands and fathers the rebellion buried among the wild aspen and poplars. He wrote in his diary, "It's as though I could hear from here the cries of the widows and orphans. I see the misery and destitution of our poor Christians. I dread hatred and revenge."

To block any more acts of revenge after Riel's execution, Grandin pleaded with government officials to pardon political prisoners, such as Poundmaker, Big Bear, Maxime Lépine and others who had received prison terms for their part in the rebellion. They were freed in 1887 after a general amnesty. But Grandin did more than feed the hungry and shelter the homeless. Once again he demonstrated his solidarity with the Metis cause by publicly placing the blame for the rebellion on the federal government's treacherous gamesmanship in dealing with the people's demands.

In an 1886 petition to the Marquess of Lansdowne, Governor-General of Canada, Grandin wrote, "I did not spare our Metis any reproaches but I would like to tell Your Honor, with all due respect, that the Canadian government must be blamed too. If I had the same authority over its members that I have over my Metis, I would tell them that more tactfully but as clearly. How many petitions and complaints did the Metis send to the government without anyone deigning to honor them with as much as an answer?"

One of the bitterest ironies of the rebellion came at the time of Riel's trial. The government commission continued its slow work of distributing land patents to Metis who qualified for them, even while the fighting was underway. By the time it was over, the Metis' demand for land, which had led to the bloodshed, was largely met.

Grandin with his nephew and niece. Joining Bishop Grandin's Western missionary work were his nephew, Oblate Father Henri Grandin, and his niece, Grey Sister Marie Heurtibise Grandin. (Courtesy Archives Deschâtelets, Ottawa)

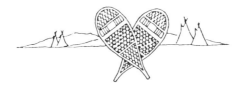

17

Old Warrior Fights On

TWO NURSING BROTHERS covered Grandin with a sheet and a blanket. Dr. Pierre Bazy moved close to the bed. "My dear Bishop, my examination shows you have stones in your bladder. They're the reason for much of your pain. I can give you some relief but only by crushing them. The operation will not be easy, I must warn you. There is some danger. I'm sure danger is nothing new to you." The doctor paused to let Grandin mull over his words.

"Today is Tuesday. If you agree, we will do the operation on Friday. Until then, get all the rest you can, in bed."

Grandin nodded agreement. "I will be ready." He had confidence in Bazy, one of the best surgeons in Paris. The bishop's nephew, Dr. Raphael Ruch, was there to assist.

Grandin could expect the Brothers of Saint John of God who ran the hospital to give him excellent care.

Once again Grandin had come to Paris for medical help, not to cure the excruciating pain but to ease it so he could continue his work. His greatest fear was that he might die far away from St. Albert, the only place he now felt at home.

The bishop opened his diary and began to write: "Thursday, Feb. 23, 1893. My room has been turned into a pharmacy, many vials filled with colored water, a lot of bandages, rubber sheets and countless kinds of surgical instruments that I hardly dare to look at.

"All this can't help but upset me. I don't think I shall sleep very much tonight. I am in God's hands. God's will be done... I accept death tomorrow or later on, according to God's good pleasure. It doesn't matter to me when or how. All I wish for is to die in his love and to be treated by him in the vastness of his forgiveness."

Grandin had written many times about death and his wish to do only God's will. He often said he was not afraid of death but of the moment after. For him, that moment could be as close as the next day. He was now sixty-four. He had been a bishop for thirty-four of those years, years of torturous travel and neglect which had left his health broken, almost beyond repair. Always, when despair threatened to engulf him, he fought off those dark moments by wrapping himself in God's forgiveness, like the blanket which protected him while he slept in a snowbank along the trail.

While God might not call immediately, Grandin did feel death edging ever closer. Each year he lost more of those dear to him. The heaviest blow had come in 1892 with the news of the death of Bishop Alexandre-Léopold Sébaux, his mentor, the man who had supported and encouraged him from his student days. Now, out of the Grandin family of thirteen children only Jean and Mélanie, his younger sister who had shared so many of the activities of his youth, were still alive.

The years should have treated Grandin more kindly but they did not. He traded his life and death struggles against flooding rivers and petrifying cold for the sophisticated fights of the boardroom and political strategies. He faced a heavy demand for churches, schools and hospitals to serve the newly arrived immigrants, and the continuing search for generous benefactors to help finance his diocese. He told his story to people in the comfortable pews of Quebec, the eastern United States and Europe, thrilling them with missionary adventures. What he failed to do was to open their wallets wide enough to pay the costs of his missionary diocese. "We cause ourselves a lot of pain and gain very little. What a job."

At five the next morning, February 24, Grandin crawled from his bed to celebrate Mass before the operation. The day was special for another reason. Thirty-nine years before, young Vital Grandin had received word he must go to the missions of the Northwest. Memories of the tearful goodbyes, the uncertainty of life in the wilderness, all these flooded his mind as he prepared to confront yet another crisis. The rest of the day was a blur. Chloroform put him to sleep but it did not kill the pain completely. He cried out several times when Dr. Bazy crushed the stones. The verdict was a partial success. With further treatment Grandin at least could resume his work with less of the crippling pain.

His old optimism quickly returned. Days later, when Bazy showed the marks on his hands from the difficult surgical procedure, the bishop joked, "See my victim." When Bazy grew concerned about some complication, Grandin tried a little therapy of his own. "Have courage, Doctor. A little more patience."

Finally, he was well enough to leave the hospital. "There is little more I can do for you, Excellency. Your life will not be easy. With care you can resume your schedule."

"Thank you, Doctor. But what about your fee? I must owe you a great deal for the operation and all the treatment."

Bazy bent to kiss Grandin's ring. "You owe me nothing, Your Excellency. Pray for me and my family. That will be payment in full."

Grandin moved in with Jean, now a canon of the cathedral of Laval. From there the bishop resumed his travels to Belgium and Rome, ready to tell his story, beg for aid and recruit new missionaries. The old campaigner did not announce his visits as his final European tour or a goodbye performance. However, that was what they turned out to be. The public goodbyes were difficult enough for one so sensitive. Most of all he dreaded the thought of the final scenes with Mélanie and Jean. His brother and sister had nurtured his every dream.

Grandin heard the huge door of St. Joseph's Church swing shut. He watched Mélanie walk slowly down the long aisle toward the altar where he prepared to celebrate his final Mass at Le Mans. The young girl who had once tended sheep with him had disappeared long ago. He had hoped the old woman approaching him might not come that morning.

"It's so early. The rain. I'd forgotten how hard it rains in France. You shouldn't..."

"Vital, stop being a bishop. Of course I came. How could I let go of this last moment with you? We are not so young any more."

He held her hand for a moment, then turned to the altar to begin the Mass. He bowed and began, "*Introibo ad altare Dei... I will go to the altar of God (Psalm 42)."* Later he wrote in his diary, "I said Mass with a lot of grief in my heart."

When the Mass was finished, the two knelt together in the damp church, the rain drumming on the stained-glass windows. Grandin led the devotional prayers for thanksgiving after Communion. They put off the moment of departure as long as they could. Without speaking, Grandin took the cross from the altar, kissed it, then held it before Mélanie. She kissed it gently, a final embrace and she was gone. He still faced one more painful farewell.

The two brothers walked hesitantly along the pier at Le Havre to the waiting ship. They talked about the day forty years before when Vital had left for North America for the first time. That was to have been their final farewell but he returned at least six times. Then, they had been young vibrant men anxious to answer God's call to serve the Church. Now the two elderly clerics walked those familiar steps to Vital's cabin one more time. The length of their years made the departure all the more difficult. Vital and Jean were certain they would never see each other again.

"Have you got all your luggage, Vital? You don't want to leave anything behind. It's a long trip back." Vital could see tears in the creases around his brother's eyes.

"I would like such an excuse. Who knows what God has in store for us? Perhaps one more time." The two men embraced. "Thank you for being such a good friend to my missions. My people bless you."

As the ship rocked gently, their wet cheeks touched for a moment. Suddenly a whistle blew, warning the passengers to leave. The two reluctantly climbed the stairs to the main deck where visitors hurried to leave the ship as the sailors made last-minute preparations before casting off.

Grandin stood with his hands on the railing, the wind puffing his white hair. He pulled his coat around his neck. The brothers waved and shouted adieu as the ship moved slowly away from the pier into the open water. Losing sight of the figure on the boat, Jean watched until the ship disappeared over the horizon. Vital stood at the railing long after the French shore became that now familiar softly pencilled line. He gave one last wave and walked below.

Back in St. Albert, April, 1894, Grandin faced the break of yet another link, the loss of his closest friend in Canada. A telegram urged him to come to St. Boniface where Archbishop Taché was dying. Grandin had stopped to visit him just six weeks before. Even then, he had seen the end quickly approaching. Grandin returned immediately to Taché's side.

"Monseigneur, I will give you absolution again. Then I will offer the holy sacrifice for you." Before Grandin could finish the celebration, Taché was dead. Grandin poured out his feelings in his diary. "Emotion is killing me, even more than work. This wonderful bishop was a father to me. His name, his authority and his writings supplied us with the greatest of services."

The funeral was hardly over before pressure began to build for Grandin's appointment as the archbishop's successor. He scoffed at the suggestion because of his age and his worsening health. Grandin was then the oldest bishop in

Canada. "Just think of it," he wrote, "I have been a bishop for thirty-seven years. The only tranfer I seek and will accept is to heaven." He began his own letter-writing campaign, corresponding with fellow bishops in Quebec, Paris and Rome. Rather than simply oppose his own appointment to St. Boniface, he argued for a coadjutor, an assistant bishop, who would share his work load in St. Albert. Three years earlier, he had convinced Pope Leo XIII to create the new diocese of Prince Albert by placing the far northern missions that belonged to the St. Albert diocese under Bishop Albert Pascal. Now he hoped the Pope would listen to his pleading, appoint a younger man with far better health as the archbishop of St. Boniface and leave the "Indian bishop" in St. Albert. Later that summer he was overjoyed with the appointment of Father Louis-Philippe-Adélard Langevin, a talented Oblate missionary, as the new archbishop of St. Boniface.

In the past Grandin had looked often for help to his friend Taché, then the archbishop of St. Boniface. Now the roles were reversed. Langevin quickly plunged into the ongoing fight for the use of the French language and the establishment of Catholic schools in Manitoba granted by the federal government but denied by Manitoba's provincial government. The bitter political battle in the Manitoba legislature, the Canadian Parliament and the Privy Council in London had hastened Taché's death. As the debate now grew more shrill, grabbing newspaper headlines day after day, Langevin buckled under the constant pressure. He complained to Grandin, "This life is unbearable. I am anxious to die. I have never been so unhappy."

Grandin forced himself to confront politicians from Macdonald down in his attempt to gain justice for his people. He learned it was a battle of wills as much as tactics. "Dear Bishop, I understand your sufferings and your worries. I share them, I assure you. But please don't let yourself get discouraged," he wrote Langevin.

The problem was not Manitoba's alone. The huge area of the Northwest Territories was an extension of Manitoba's linguistic and religious battleground. For half a century European civilization had moved across the plains mainly as French and Catholic. Now, immigrants who spoke many languages and worshipped in other churches challenged the French fact. Grandin knew the story well. Politicians made promises at election time. Delivery was seldom quick. How he had looked with hope to the proclamation of 1869 that guaranteed the continuation of all civil and religious privileges in the territories. In effect, Catholics and Protestants should enjoy the same rights. Eight years later, the French language was added to the guarantee of religious education. But by 1889 opponents to the use of French in the territories' council moved to eliminate it for practical reasons: the cost of printing documents in both English and French was too high. The Church too lost much of its control over Catholic schools through a shift in decision-making power. Grandin shook his head in disbelief at the twisted position politicians could take to win votes. English-speaking politicians, like Edward Blake, a Protestant, supported the rights of the French minorities. At the same time, Wilfrid Laurier, a Catholic, a Quebec politician and future Canadian prime minister, was cool toward French rights.

Grandin interpreted the political moves as a direct attack on the Church and an attempt to undermine the influence of the missionaries. When officials of the Bureau of Indian Affairs refused food to Catholic residents at the Thunderchild reserve, because they would not enrol their children at the Protestant school, he decided it was time for another trip to the prime minister's office.

Macdonald turned on the charm when Grandin threatened to take his grievances to the newspapers. He invited the bishop to his home for dinner and he sent a plush coach with uniformed footmen. "Never did I accept a dinner and honors with so much repugnance," Grandin wrote. The meeting in 1890 produced an immediate written agreement recognizing Grandin's school at Lac La Biche and a promise for two new industrial schools at Duck Lake in present-day Saskatchewan and Onion Lake northeast of Edmonton, plus the right of missionaries to work on reserves.

The fight for full exercise of the right to French Catholic schools preoccupied Grandin throughout much of the 1890s. He wrote letters, made representations, pleaded with politicians to keep their promises. Pope Leo XIII supported

Grandin and the other Canadian bishops, condemning the public schools which he saw as morally neutral and without a religious basis. He sent a personal representative, Cardinal Raphael Merry Del Val, to negotiate a settlement with the federal government. Despite more promises, nothing came of all this effort. Just as Grandin had bluntly expressed his feelings to Macdonald when he disagreed with federal policy, he did not spare the new prime minister. Grandin laid out in detail the injustices of the education system for Sir Wilfrid Laurier. For one who had fought so hard, half measures were not enough. Grandin expected Laurier to keep his word in full.

"I take the liberty to add, Right Honorable Sir Wilfrid, that bishops are not the only ones who will have to render an account to God for their actions."

Strongly worded letters and desk pounding were not enough to overcome the hard fact that the French language and Catholic schools were no longer the choice of the majority of people. If only he could persuade young Quebeckers to move West rather than emigrate to the United States, perhaps there would be enough French-speaking settlers at least to make the politicians take notice. Grandin tried to persuade his brother bishops in Quebec to encourage their adventurous young people to consider life in the West. The answer — they were not ready to see their future sacrificed to populate the empty plains. Grandin did not give up without an argument.

"How many thousands of your young people move to the United States every year? Many of them not only lose their souls but their health as well. They're lost to your province and to the Dominion... If only for the last ten years one-quarter of your people who went to the United States had come West, we might still be in the majority. At least we would be a large enough minority so there would no question of not making special laws for us."

Although he did not receive the kind of response he wanted, Grandin would not quit trying. He launched his own settlement program and sent Father Lacombe to Quebec. Lacombe's reputation in the West made him a celebrity in Eastern Canada. Working with Father Jean-Baptiste Morin, the two men attracted enough French-speaking settlers to establish several new communities: Morinville and Legal north of Edmonton, and Beaumont to the south of the city.

Religious congregations at last began to show interest in his diocese. Grandin rejoiced when the Sisters of the Assumption of the Blessed Virgin from Nicolet, Quebec, considered working in Edmonton. "Come for God alone. Come and win souls... To do good for the Indians you will have to love them and sacrifice yourselves for them. Don't count on their gratitude."

The mother general of the congregation, Mère Sainte-Marie (Mathilde Leduc), asked for time to think and pray on this critical decision which would take her sisters to the back trails of the Northwest, a world away from the cobble-stoned streets of Montreal. When there was no final decision after four months of prayer and careful consideration, Grandin wrote to her, "You are quite right, my Reverend Mother, to consult God in prayer, but you must not count on a direct revelation." The sisters came.

After more than four decades of a simple self-sacrificing lifestyle, the practical expression of his vow of poverty, Grandin accepted some relaxation of the strict rules which set the routine of his life. In 1892, Father Lacombe organized a trip for seven Western bishops to visit a festival of Catholic Indians in British Columbia. On their way they stopped to enjoy Grandin's hospitality. He treated the visit as a great occasion. For the first time in his residence he allowed the brothers to put sheets on the beds and a sugar bowl on the table. The bowl reappeared occasionally after the visitors had left. The incident showed that the harsh life was changing.

The pressures increased on Grandin as the 1890s passed. His diocese needed more schools and hospitals and he juggled his meager resources to plan new institutions. By 1897 the diocese was divided into five districts: St. Albert, Edmonton, Calgary, Saddle Lake, and the Blackfeet nation in southern Alberta, with a total of sixty-five missions. In 1898, four Sisters of Misericordia and a nurse arrived to establish the Misericordia Hospital, the second hospital in Edmonton, just a block from the Grey Nuns General Hospital.

The man who had slept in snowbanks and dipped his fingers into a common pot to share the evening meal of his Indian friends strained to discover what God's providence might have in store for his diocese. He worried that the Church's influence was waning as other denominations, politicians and government officials were exercising more control. Grandin wanted the diocese to pass into the hands of a capable new bishop before his death.

18

I Belong to God

THE PEN scratched out line after line across the paper. At last Grandin had a helper, a coadjutor bishop, someone to carry on after his death. Thanks be to God and to Pope Leo. Quickly, he must tell the good news to his people. Without warning, a coughing spasm racked his frail body. He reached for a glass of water sitting on the table that was his desk. At dinner he told his priests and brothers, "This good news makes me forget how tired and sick I am."

He put down his pen. He wanted to reflect on his words, to hear how they sounded, the words he had longed to write for so many years. His thin delicate fingers held the paper close to his eyes in the May twilight. "As you know, old age, sickness and the infirmities that come with it have made us unable for quite some time to carry out the duties of our office. As long as these were only difficult, it was for us a real comfort to perform them..." The 1897 pastoral letter was like a will, an outpouring of Grandin's love for the people he would serve for another five years until his death.

"This man who has been named by our Holy Father acting on God's behalf, upon our request, which was supported by our beloved metropolitan and the other bishops of our province, is Bishop Émile-Joseph Légal... We doubt whether Bishop Légal will be able to love you more than we, but we can assure that he will love just as much.

"And you to whom we write, perhaps for the last time, you will love him as you have loved us, for he is the one chosen by God. He is our brother and, as we hope to have the privilege of imposing our hands on him, our son." Grandin did consecrate the new bishop and his successor, June 17, 1897.

Father Légal put his tools down when he received work of his appointment as a bishop. He had just finished making a coffin for a young girl who had suddenly died. During his sixteen years with the Blackfeet in the south, he had served the people every way he could. The Blackfeet called him "Sportsitapi," The One Sitting Above. He was their teacher, doctor, even gravedigger. The Blackfeet generally resisted the missionaries' attempts to make them Christians. But even when Grandin asked him to move to other, easier missions, the priest would not abandon the people. Always his answer was the same. "I prefer to stay among my Indians, despite the little profit my ministry brings and the sterility of all our efforts. It will take years, generations perhaps, to transform these nations. Some missionaries have to be present during these sterile and unsuccessful years. I have no objection to being one of them." Despite his wish to remain with the Blackfeet, when the episcopal call came, Émile-Joseph Légal could not refuse.

For Grandin, the freedom from weeks of travel and daily demands was a tonic. His spirit and walk regained some of their vigor. "Émile, sit down for a few minutes. We don't get much time to talk." Grandin pushed back the chair from his table and waited until Légal was settled. "I must go to

St. Boniface to discuss the problem of the Galicians with Archbishop Langevin. They're arriving by the train load from Europe. Already there are 30,000 in the West. Many come with hardly enough clothes."

"Yes, our priests complain many of the other immigrants won't accept the Galicians. They look down on these people with their different customs as, well, even worse than the Indians."

"What about the more serious religious problem?" Grandin leaned forward to hear what Légal had learned.

"They have the idea we want to change them from Greek Catholics to Latin Catholics, destroy all their customs, their language as well. For that reason they won't have anything to do with our priests."

"Émile, we must make it clear we don't want to make them members of our congregations, somehow to Latinize them. Our priests must understand this too."

"The only answer is to find them priests of their own, priests of the Greek rite," Légal said.

"Yes, I agree. I will take that message to the archbishop. Perhaps he has contacts in Europe to get them priests."

The problem proved far harder to solve than the two St. Albert bishops imagined. After several unsuccessful attempts to persuade priests to move from Europe to serve the Galicians or Ukrainian Catholics, as they are known today, Grandin sent Father Lacombe in 1898 to ask for help directly from Emperor Franz Joseph and the Austrian bishops. When there was no immediate prospect of new priests, he sent Father Alphonse Jan, an Oblate who was trying to serve the Galicians in the Edmonton area, to make another attempt the next year to get Ukrainian-speaking priests from Europe. Jan's efforts resulted in an agreement with the Reformed Basilian Fathers of Galicia to send priests to Canada to minister to the Ukrainian pioneers.

Grandin and Légal put aside their problems briefly in 1899 to mark one of the most important jubilees in the history of St. Albert — Father Lacombe's fifty years as a priest. The invitations went out to celebrate September 25 as "Father

Lacombe Day." Congratulations arrived from remote missions, government offices and Indian reservations from across the country and overseas, honoring the man the Crees called "Noble Soul." Speakers hailed his five decades of dedication to the native people and the new settlers.

Grandin added his toast to complete the day of thanksgiving for this remarkable man. He spoke not so much as a bishop praising one of his priests but with the warmth of two friends and partners united in the work of half a century. "Whenever a mediator, a spokesman, was needed to approach the government, the Canadian Pacific Railway or for any other significant mission, everyone asked me for Father Lacombe. He has given to everyone."

Grandin explained why Lacombe had never become a bishop, as many expected him to be. The missionary preferred to roam the West and beyond, going where he was most needed. "God, who runs everything with wisdom, wanted him to be free, to be available for everything and to everyone."

The celebration ended with fireworks blazing across the St. Albert sky, a spectacular display many had never seen before. For Grandin, the short-lived brilliance was a poignant sign. "All worldly glory passes," he wrote. "Father Lacombe's jubilee is over; all those who came solely for the celebration have left us. The celebrations, however beautiful they may have been, have disappeared, like the fireworks that were launched last night. All that is left is the memory. It is the same with life; a rocket that reaches different heights follows a curve, then soon disappears after giving some light. Most often it emphasizes only the night's darkness."

During his final days, Grandin appeared driven to use every moment to complete his life's work. It was most obvious in his dealings with his priests. He wrote to one, "My dear friend, the one thing you must dread is mediocrity because it deprives us of the gifts of the Holy Spirit. We are poor, worthless, puny; let us at least be generous, men with large, noble souls. We are few; our virtues must supply for numbers. Let us always say yes to God's inspirations and no to our human inclinations."

Yet Grandin displayed a balance in his rush to complete God's work. He wrote to another of his priests, "You must take care of yourself. It seems to me that a person can be zealous without killing himself. Since God chooses to make use of us, it is our duty not to impair our health or ruin it. A poor man who earns his daily bread with one horse might, for a time, make more money by working the horse day and night, but the horse would soon die and the man would lose more than he had gained. We must take care of our bodies because we need them in order to work for God."

He took his own advice. Less responsibility gave him time to enjoy special St. Albert celebrations like the blessing of the minor seminary and the dedication of the cornerstone for a new cathedral.

There were embarrassing moments too. After more than forty years as a bishop, Grandin still did not like attention being showered on him. One night after dinner, Bishop Légal invited him into the common room where the priests and brothers gathered. Father Lacombe stood while Grandin eased himself into a chair.

"My dear Bishop," Lacombe began. "We have a gift for you. We hope you will accept it with the good wishes of the priests and religious of your diocese and the members of your family." With a flourish Lacombe pulled a cloth from the gift, revealing a white plaster bust of Grandin. The bishop scowled while the others applauded and nodded their approval. Grandin had forbidden Lacombe to consider allowing a sculptor to make a bust of him when it had been first proposed several years before. Surely there were enough photographs, even a portrait to remind them of what he looked like! Grandin accepted the gift graciously. He did not want to hurt Lacombe's feelings.

"They should have abstained from this misplaced luxury for me," he wrote. If he were a celebrated bishop, rather than the beggar bishop as he was known, it might have been acceptable. "I call it a folly. I regret it sincerely."

The saddest moment came with the delivery of a terse telegram just fourteen months before his own death. "Canon dead. Signed : Frédéric Grandin." His sister Mélanie had died a few months before. Now Vital was the only surviving member of thirteen children. With Jean's death, the diocese lost a missionary who never had left his French home but who constantly told Vital's heroic story to everyone who would listen and help.

Despite his rapidly failing health, Grandin set an example for the Oblates who shared the St. Albert residence with him. Every morning before the others were out of bed, he was in the chapel making the Way of the Cross. In the final few weeks of his life he dragged himself from one station of the cross to the next on his knees. He prayed far into the night before the tabernacle.

The pain from his ailments could not keep him from his daily routine of prayer. "For fifty years I have made my morning meditation every day. I fear I have not made it satisfactorily once. How many distractions at times! I hope to make up for this in heaven," he wrote in his diary.

The priests and brothers watched the ordeal of his final days unfold. Whispered stories of his patience and humor made the rounds. "It is good to live with Bishop Grandin," an elderly brother repeated often. They also saw his temper flare whenever the Church or the Oblates were challenged. Just as quickly, he apologized or showered some kindness to repair any hurt feelings. Right to his final year of life he continued the practice of renewing his vows at New Year's, although as a bishop he was no longer bound by the Oblate rule. "Today, as I have done every year, I have with great joy renewed my vows on my bended knees and in spirit placed myself at the Father General's feet."

By the end of January, 1902, Grandin could no longer celebrate Mass. Two weeks later, he suffered an attack few thought he would survive. Father Leduc gave him the Eucharist and anointed him, yet he rallied, despite intense suffering from his stomach and other ailments. Active work in the diocese was no longer possible but he maintained a strong interest in the events and decisions of the Church, now in the twentieth century. One of his last public appearances came April 6 in St. Albert at the consecration of Bishop Gabriel Breynat, the new head of the northern diocese of Mackenzie.

Grandin struggled out of bed to meet the six visiting bishops and to have his picture taken with them.

By June 2, having grown dangerously weak, he asked Bishop Légal to administer the last sacraments and to call his friends for a final visit. The word spread through the mission. "The bishop is dying." Silently, the priests and brothers, Grey Nuns from the convent and employees of the mission gathered in Grandin's room.

His niece, Sister Marie Heurtebise Grandin, stood close to her uncle. When he heard that Father Henri Grandin, his nephew, could not arrive that day because of the muddy roads, Vital accepted the news with the resignation he always showed to disappointment. "That is another sacrifice he and I will offer to God." Outside his window, robins and sparrows chirped and chattered with new life to greet the beautiful June day. New green leaves fluttered in the soft wind. Inside, his life ebbing away, Grandin urged his Oblate family and others kneeling at his bedside to continue their half century of work.

Bishop Légal described the scene. "He spoke to us for about ten minutes and then his strength failed him. He begged pardon of any he might have offended. He thanked all his priests, brothers, sisters, the Oblate congregation and all his benefactors for what they had done for him and for the diocese... and then he blessed them."

After a brief rest to regain some strength, Grandin renewed his vows of poverty, chastity, obedience and the Oblate vow of perseverance for life, "so help me God." Once he had received the Eucharist and the sacrament of the sick, a slow procession moved past his bedside. Each one embraced him for the last time. He comforted them and offered an encouraging word. During the day some came back to his room for personal talks. Sister Marie visited him several times and they discussed their relatives in France. Vital Grandin passed on advice about their lives and gave suggestions to make them happier.

Later that evening Sister Cécilia Wagner, one of the Grey Nuns who was nursing Grandin, answered a knock on the front door. "Doctor Blais, I was just going to call you. The bishop is much weaker than he was when you were here earlier. I doubt he will live through the night."

Aristide Blais threw his hat on a chair in the hallway and followed her to the bishop's bedroom. When the specialist entered the dimly lit room, the priests and brothers who had grouped around the bishop's bed moved aside. At Sister Wagner's suggestion they left the room to let Blais examine his patient.

Grandin was calm as the doctor reached for his wrist to take his pulse. "How is your pain, Excellency?"

"About the same. Sometimes a little worse, then a little better."

"I have some medicine in my bag that would help to relieve it. If only you give permission. I know your feelings."

Grandin's lips moved but Blais could not make out his words. He leaned closer, his ear just a few inches from the bishop's mouth. "The medicine is not necessary, Doctor. I accept my pain."

Blais squeezed Grandin's hand, then turned away to speak to Sister Marie. She looked into his eyes as he shook his head. "I don't understand how he can bear the pain. He has a general infection of his urinary system. His temperature is high; the heartbeat is rapid and irregular. It is only a matter of hours. I know you will do what you can to make him more comfortable. I only wish he would allow me to give him something for the pain."

"He lived his life in pain. Every suffering was for God. You can't expect him to change now."

The doctor returned to the patient's bedside and knelt before Grandin. "Excellency, if you are strong enough, may I have your blessing?" Grandin traced the sign of the cross, the words only a whisper.

"We wished to sit up in turns with him during the night but he felt this was unnecessary. Brother Auguste Landais, who had nursed him during his illness, spent the night alone with him," Légal wrote.

Grandin lost consciousness about three in the morning. Légal rushed to his bedside to spend the final moments with him. Grandin regained consciousness but the pain was unbearable. His loud moans rose and fell throughout the house. "Jesus, Mary and Joseph," he repeated many times. His final agony began about five o'clock. The community members again knelt around his bedside. He kissed his Oblate cross. Father Michel Merer, his confessor, gave him the final blessing. There was a murmur of prayers to God to ease the bishop's suffering.

"I began the prayers for the dying. Just before I had finished them, Bishop Grandin stopped breathing. His beautiful soul had gone to God; his journey over, he found rest."

Streaks of red already colored the northeastern sky over St. Albert as the church bells tolled the news of the bishop's death. Men and women, crawling from their warm beds in the farmhouses along the Sturgeon River, knew immediately their friend and bishop was dead. For five days people shuffled slowly down the main aisle of the cathedral past the coffin to pray in Grandin's sight for one last time. Indians and Metis, whom he loved as his brothers and sisters, immigrants from Europe, the leaders and the least significant of the Northwest came out of respect and love for the man who had been one of them. They brought rosaries, medals, every kind of religious article to touch Grandin's hands and the worn cassock he had asked to be buried in. They wanted to preserve some link with him that could touch and bless their lives.

"*Requiem aeternam dona eis, Domine...* Eternal rest grant to them, O Lord." On June 10, Bishop Légal began the solemn funeral Mass as rain pounded against the windows and the roof of the cathedral. The crowd overflowed the church down the steps to the brink of the hill overlooking the Sturgeon Valley. The mourners huddled together for protection from the fierce June storm. They would not leave the bishop they deeply loved.

Once the Mass was finished and the five traditional absolutions given, several men lowered the coffin into a temporary grave in front of the sanctuary. There it would remain until the new cathedral was completed with a crypt that eventually would hold Grandin's tomb and those of Fathers Lacombe and Leduc. The bishop's body was moved March 19, 1906, to its present resting place in what is now the St. Albert parish church. The headquarters of the diocese were moved to nearby Edmonton in 1912 and so the St. Albert diocese became the Edmonton archdiocese.

On February 24, 1937, thirty-five years after his death, the decree for the introduction of Grandin's cause for beatification was issued in Rome by the Vatican. Vital Justin Grandin was declared venerable in 1966. Today, the work is continuing for his beatification with the hope he will one day be canonized and declared a saint.

In a statement that served as his will, Grandin revealed the spirit that inspired him in life and which continues to make him powerful in death.

"Since I am a religious and a missionary, I live and do good only through charitable donations. I have absolutely nothing to bequeath, nothing belongs to me personally. I myself belong to God and I am entirely his thing... Should I die while visiting my diocese but not at an Oblate mission, I desire that to continue preaching the mystery of the redemption a large wooden cross be erected where I die.

"Should I be drowned, I wish that a cross be erected where the accident occurred or where my body is found. I wish to be robed in old vestments and to be buried in a plain coffin made by one of our brothers. The only favor I ask of God is that I die in his love and that he judge me with great mercy."

Notes

Chapter 1

Vital Grandin's dramatic brush with death on two occasions within a few weeks in the winter of 1863-64 was first described in detail by Rev. E. Jonquet in *Mgr Grandin* (Montreal: 1903). There are few comprehensive works in English on Grandin's life. Two sources are Rev. Léon Hermant, *Thy Cross My Stay* (Toronto: 1948) and M. B. Venini Byrne, *From the Buffalo to the Cross* (Calgary: 1973).

The bishop's diary is only now being translated by personnel at the Provincial Archives of Alberta from the original French into English. His many letters to his family and friends during his almost half century in Canada have been partially translated into English by Rev. Antonio Duhaime, OMI, of St. Albert, vice-postulator in charge of Grandin's cause for canonization.

Chapters 2, 3 and 4

Grandin's boyhood and teenage years illustrate the mysterious ways in which God calls people to a particular vocation. It would have been so easy for young Vital to conclude God did not want him to be a priest and least of all a missionary in a foreign land. His three biographers, Jonquet, Hermant and Rev. P. E. Breton (*Vital Grandin, O.M.I.* [Paris: 1960]) show the struggle Grandin endured.

Grandin's meeting with Bishop Alexandre-Antonin Taché and their lifelong friendship demonstrates how other people can change the direction of our lives. Taché was another of the first great Oblate missionaries to come to Western Canada. Born in Fraserville, Quebec, 1823, he became one of the first Canadian Oblate novices and was the first priest ordained west of the Great Lakes. Just three years after his ordination as a priest, he became at the age of 27 coadjutor bishop of St. Boniface. In 1853 he succeeded Joseph Norbert Provencher as bishop of the huge diocese which stretched to the Rocky Mountains and the North Pole. St. Boniface became an archdiocese in 1871.

Chapter 5

Nativity Mission is on the northwest shore of Lake Athabasca at the pioneer settlement of Fort Chipewyan, one of the important links in the Hudson's Bay Company's trading network. Travel to such missions was long and difficult as Grandin soon learned. Coupled with the almost complete lack of privacy, Grandin's shy nature and the approach to modesty taught in European seminaries made frontier travel that much harder for him.

Chapter 6

Grandin admired the dedication of the fur traders and the zeal of the men who operated the Hudson's Bay Company forts but was critical of what he considered to be their exploitation of and lack of concern for the majority of the Indians. Peter C. Newman in his *Company of Adventurers*, volume 1 (Markham, Ont. : 1985), calls the Indians the "ghosts of Canadian history." According to Newman, they were part of the background, not so much abused as ignored. He points out that the Indians were far more sophisticated traders than the furs-for-trinkets image given by history books would suggest.

From Grandin's viewpoint, the Indians were the losers in the clash of cultures. Unhappy that the traders did not recognize what was obvious to the missionaries, Grandin saw the HBC as hostile to the French Catholic Oblates. However, evidence shows that at times the HBC preferred Roman Catholic to Anglican and Protestant missionaries because the former were neither accompanied by nor responsible for wives and children. Events in Grandin's life also show that the bishop and the Hudson's Bay traders did co-operate on many occasions when language and religious differences had to be forgotten simply to survive the harsh climate and the frontier conditions.

The missionaries were greatly disturbed by actions of the Indians which the priests perceived as cruelty. Men of certain tribes are recorded to have considered the killing of children and women as necessary at times. Jonquet states (p. 71, translated from the original French) :

"It was not infrequent to see a husband kill his wife when he felt the need to get rid of her. All these horrors seemed so natural that the poor Indian women looked upon themselves as destined to suffer them...

"But thanks to the Gospel, everything changed : mothers, wives soon recovered their rights. An Indian, struck by a teaching, went to Father Grandin and told him, '... When you told us that the Son of God had taken a mother among women, it became quite clear to me that women have a soul and a heaven like men.' "

Chapter 7

One of Grandin's strengths was his determination to face any challenge that threatened the physical or spiritual well-being of the Indian. He would not tolerate what he considered to be a false prophet leading his people away from the Catholic faith. In this case, the Montagnais' whole way of life with their few possessions was in danger. This same attitude surfaced in Grandin's relationships both with other denominations working to convert the Indians and with government leaders in their dealings with the Indians over land and schools.

Despite his personal reluctance to undertake the responsibilities of a bishop, Grandin's determination to do what was right, no matter what the cost, and his concern for the Indians served him well and made him an ideal person to guide the growth and development of the struggling Church in the West.

Chapter 8

There was none of today's ecumenical spirit between the Oblate missionaries and the ministers of the Anglican and Protestant denominations in the West. They viewed each other as doing the devil's work. The hostile attitudes caused many tensions and conflicts which would take decades to heal.

Rev. Claude Champagne, *Les débuts de la mission dans le Nord-Ouest canadien* (Ottawa : 1983), footnote 180, pp. 88-89, cites some revealing quotations from English documents showing the depth of the interdenominational hostility and the excesses of language which would be unthinkable today.

Grandin's careful choice of Providence Mission prepared the way in 1862 for dividing the huge St. Boniface diocese. The northern missions were grouped together to form the vicariate of Athabasca-Mackenzie under the direction of Bishop Henri Faraud.

Chapter 9

Baptizing Indians who embraced the faith was an important function of the Catholic missionaries but they have also been criticized for being too hasty to baptize.

Father Champagne, of the Institute of Mission Studies, St. Paul University, Ottawa, made the following observation to this author :

"For their part, Grandin and the missionaries of his diocese baptized, as a rule, every child that was presented to them. Whether the child's parents were Catholic, Protestant, catechumen or non-Christian was of little or no consequence, as the missionaries were primarily concerned with the high infant mortality rate. Baptism also had the effect of establishing a special relationship between the children and the Church (this was true for Protestants and Anglicans as well as Catholics).

"Adult baptism presupposed knowledge of the principal mysteries of faith and the prayers necessary for the recitation of the rosary, and a Christian lifestyle. The missionaries demanded less from the sick."

Chapters 10 and 11

Readers can find more details about the early struggles to establish the new diocese of St. Albert and the community which grew around the St. Albert mission in two books by Émile Tardif, OMI, written for the centennial of what is today the city of St. Albert : *Saint Albert* and *Centenaire de Saint-Albert ; Saint Albert Centennial : 1861-1961* (Edmonton : 1961).

Chapter 12

Father Albert Lacombe (1827-1916), originally from St. Sulpice, Quebec, was a dominant figure in the growth of the Church in the West. Grandin saved the most difficult assignments for the more outgoing Lacombe who had Indian blood and understood the Indian mentality. P. E. Breton, *The Big Chief of the Prairies: The Life of Father Lacombe*, translated by Hugh A. Dempsey (Montreal : Fides, 1956), and James G. MacGregor, *Father Lacombe* (Edmonton : Hurtig Publishers, © 1975), tell the fascinating story of Grandin's confrere.

Chapters 13 and 14

Wherever missions were established in the West, the Grey Nuns arrived soon after to provide hospitals and schools for the native and white population. They provided the only social services in the huge territory until the Faithful Companions of Jesus, the Sisters of the Assumption and the Sisters of Misericordia arrived. M. B. Venini Byrne, *From the Buffalo to the Cross*, gives some details of the great work done by sisters in the Calgary diocese.

Chapters 15, 16 and 17

Sir John A. Macdonald, Canada's first prime minister, was Grandin's main opponent in his continuing fight for French-language rights, Catholic schools, and fair land settlements for the Indians and Metis. Donald Swainson, *John A. Macdonald, the Man and the Politician* (Toronto : 1971), gives the background to the new country and its politics. A recent book by Nicholas Tkach, *Alberta Catholic Schools, A Social History* (Edmonton : University of Alberta Publication Services, 1983), traces the development of the province's Catholic school system.

The Riel Rebellion of 1885 was the culmination of the Indian and Metis grievances against the federal government and Prime Minister Macdonald in particular. Grandin and his missionaries supported the native claims but would not become involved in violence. The rebellion and its damaging effect on the relationship between the missionaries and the Indians and Metis is a complex story. *Prairie Fire: The 1885 North-West Rebellion* by Bob Beal and R.C. MacLeod (Edmonton : Hurtig Publishers, 1985) and *Strange Empire : A Narrative of the Northwest* by Joseph Kinsey Howard (New York : 1952), fill in the details of this significant event in Canadian history.

Chapter 18

Grandin's final days ended just the way he lived his whole life. Continuing to disregard his own pain, his attention was focused on what he believed was God's will for him and the problems of those around him. In a brief written statement which forms part of this chapter, Dr. (later Senator) Aristide Blais of St. Albert provided this insight into Grandin's last hours :

After a lifetime of illness, the bishop finally died of blood poisoning of the urinary system, "a very serious and painful disease which very often develops into swelling of the prostate gland, eventually causing total obstruction... We joined in prayer with the faithful of his diocese for the intentions of this holy man who, vested in his sacerdotal vestments, went straight to the heavens of the blessed."

Bibliography

BEAL, Bob and R. C. MacLEOD. *Prairie Fire: The 1885 North-West Rebellion.* Edmonton: Hurtig Publishers, 1985.

BRETON, P. E. *Vital Grandin, O.M.I.: la merveilleuse aventure de "l'évêque sauvage" des Prairies et du Grand Nord.* Préface de Daniel-Rops. Bibliothèque Ecclesia, 58. Paris: Librairie A. Fayard, 1960.

BYRNE, M. B. Venini. *From the Buffalo to the Cross: A History of the Roman Catholic Diocese of Calgary.* Calgary: Calgary Archives and Historical Publications, 1973.

CHAMPAGNE, Claude. *Les débuts de la mission dans le Nord-Ouest canadien: mission et église chez Mgr Vital Grandin, O.M.I., 1829-1902.* Ottawa: Éditions de l'Université St-Paul, 1983. Doctoral thesis, Gregorian University, Rome.

FUMOLEAU, René. *As Long As This Land Shall Last: A History of Treaty 8 and Treaty 11, 1870-1939.* Toronto: McClelland and Stewart, 1973.

GRAY, James H. *Booze: The Impact of Whisky on the Prairie West.* Toronto: Macmillan of Canada, 1972.

HERMANT, Léon. *Thy Cross My Stay: The Life of the Servant of God Vital Justin Grandin, Oblate of Mary Immaculate and First Bishop of St. Albert, Canada.* Toronto: The Mission Press, 1948.

HOWARD, Joseph Kinsey. *Strange Empire: A Narrative of the Northwest.* New York: W. Morrow, 1952.

JONQUET, E. *Mgr Grandin: Oblat de Marie Immaculée, premier évêque de Saint-Albert.* Montreal, 1903.

LANGER, William L., ed. *Western Civilization*, vol. 1: *The Struggle for Empire to Europe in the Modern World.* Harper-American Heritage Textbook. New York: American Heritage Publishing Co., 1968.

MacGREGOR, James G. *Edmonton: A History.* Edmonton: Hurtig Publishers, 1967.

NEWMAN, Peter C. *Company of Adventurers*, vol. 1. Markham, Ont.: Viking, 1985.

PALMER, Howard and Tamara Jeppson PALMER. *Peoples of Alberta: Portraits of Cultural Diversity.* Saskatoon: Western Producer Prairie Books, 1985.

PRICE, Richard, ed. *The Spirit of the Alberta Indian Treaties.* Montreal: Institute for Research on Public Policy/Institut de recherches politiques, 1979.

SWAINSON, Donald. *John A. Macdonald, the Man and the Politician.* Canadian Lives. Toronto: Oxford University Press, 1971.

TARDIF, Émile. *Centenaire de Saint-Albert; Saint Albert Centennial, 1861-1961.* Edmonton: Imprimerie La Survivance Ltée., 1961.

_____. *Saint Albert.* Edmonton: Imprimerie La Survivance, 1961.

TÉTRAULT, Georges, comp. *Oblates at Rest: Life and Work Sketches of the Oblate Missionaries in the Saint Albert Cemetery.* Edited by Antonio Duhaime. Edmonton: Inland Printing Ltd., 1983.

Index